Anna, Countess of the Covenant

Mary McGrigor grew up in a 15th-century Scottish castle which inspired her love of history. When she was twenty she married Sir Charles McGrigor, who eventually retired to become a hill farmer in Argyll. Inspired by local artefacts she wrote a number of local histories before branching out into articles for *Scottish Field*. Her book *Argyll, Land of Blood and Beauty* published in 2000, was followed by others including historical biographies, this being her fourth. She lives near Port Sonachan in Argyll.

Anna, Countess of the Covenant

A MEMOIR OF LADY ANNA MACKENZIE
COUNTESS OF BALCARRES AND
AFTERWARDS COUNTESS OF ARGYLL

Mary McGrigor

BIRLINN

First published in 2008 by
Birlinn Limited
West Newington House
10 Newington Road
Edinburgh
EH9 1QS

www.birlinn.co.uk

ISBN 13: 978 1 84158 668 7
ISBN 10: 1 84158 668 4

British Library Cataloguing-in-Publication Data
A catalogue record for this book is available from the British Library

Typeset by Iolaire Typesetting, Newtonmore
Printed and bound by Cox & Wyman Ltd, Reading, Berkshire

To my wonderful family
and to the doctors and staff of
Lorn and the Isles Hospital and the
Victoria Infirmary, with my deep gratitude

Contents

―――▶◀―――

Contents

List of Illustrations

Maps

0 50 100 150 Kilometres

0 50 100 Miles

ORKNEY
ISLANDS
• Kirkwall

LEWIS

HARRIS

SKYE

Brahan Castle • • Cromarty
R. Conon
• Inverness

R. Spey

R. Don
R. Dee • Aberdeen

LOCHABER

MULL

R. Tay
• Dundee
R. Forth • St Andrews
Carnasserie Castle • Stirling • • Balcarres
NORTH SEA
Falkirk •
ISLAY • Greenock • • Glasgow
• Edinburgh
KINTYRE *R. Clyde*
R. Tweed
Campbeltown •

• Newcastle

• Carlisle

IRISH SEA

York •

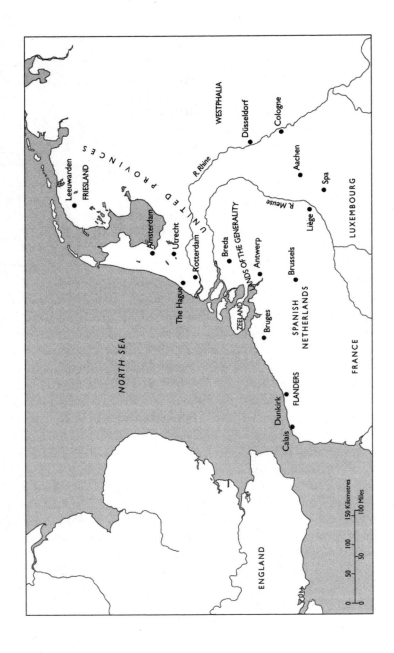

The Hard-fought Land

———————

The River Conon rises in the mountains of Wester Ross and flows east to the Cromarty Firth running almost from coast to coast. The upper reaches are turbulent. The stream, foaming white after heavy rain lashing against great mountains, plunges through gorges and down waterfalls to reach a wider stretch of the glen. Here there used to be dry stone cottages thatched with turf, the cattle in the byre at one end. Today there are only ruins below the water of the loch, created when the river was dammed by the North of Scotland Hydro Board shortly after the Second World War. Below the dam the Conon flows through a wide strath of fertile ground, where sheep and cattle now graze peacefully on land that has been largely cleared of stones. Here, on a field called the Park, just above the north bank, a party of MacDonalds returning from a raid on the Black Isle with much spoil, were surprised and nearly annihilated by the MacKenzies in 1493. The battle was significant in that it resulted eventually in the resignation of his vast territory by John MacDonald, Lord of the Isles, to the young King James IV.

A hundred years later it was Kenneth, Lord Kintail, chief of the Mackenzies, who became the predator when, by devious means, he acquired the Isle of Lewis and the district of Gairloch on the nearby western coast from the people who had held these lands from before recorded time, the Clan Macleod.

It was into this world that Lady Anna Mackenzie was born, in 1621. Her parents were Colin, Lord Kintail, and his wife

Margaret Seton, daughter of the Earl of Dunfermline, Chancellor of Scotland. It was largely thanks to the influence of his father-in-law and to his association with King James VI of Scotland, who became James I of England in 1603, that at the time of his daughter's birth, Kintail was one of the most powerful nobles in Scotland, surpassed only in importance by Archibald Campbell, 8th Earl of Argyll.

In 1623 Colin Mackenzie, Lord of Kintail, achieved even greater prominence when he was created Earl of Seaforth by the king. The rents he received from the huge stretch of territory over which he held sway made him a very rich man. Although some of his fortune vanished in a dispute with Argyll over the superiority of Moidart and Arisaig, he was ultimately successful in winning his claim, thereby further extending the territory over which he could summon men to arms.

Thus, with these latest additions, together with the Western Isles of Lewis and Harris, Seaforth held an enormous belt of land stretching across the northern part of Scotland from the west coast to the east.

Argyll likewise, although reluctantly relinquishing Moidart and Arisaig, had greatly increased his sphere of influence through the acquisition of the island of Islay and of the mainland peninsula of Kintyre. Hereditary possessions of Sir James MacDonald of Dunyveg, these lands had been forfeited to the crown after his failed rebellion of 1615 and had subsequently been granted to Argyll.

Little could anyone at that time have guessed how these territorial transactions would influence the life of the little girl called Anna, at that time just two years old.

PART I

CHAPTER I

Child to the Castle Born

Colin Mackenzie, 1ˢᵗ Earl of Seaforth, known as Colin Ruadh, Colin the red, for the colour of his hair, was as different in character from his predatory ancestors as the proverbial chalk and cheese.

His mind having been widened by travel on the Continent he determined, on returning to Ross-shire, to civilise the local people. To this purpose he provided for the kirks in Lewis and elsewhere and gave 'valuable books from London, the works of the latest and best authors' to churches within his sphere. Aware of the value of education, he gave 4,000 merks to the grammar school of Chanonry, where boys whose homes were far away could board.[1]

As might be expected of a man of such standing, Colin made what was probably an arranged marriage, with Lady Margaret Seton, daughter of his father's old friend and compatriot, the lawyer Alexander Seton, Earl of Dunfermline since 1605. His bride had significant connections, one sister, Sophia, being married to David, Lord Lindsay of Balcarres, and another, Isabel, to John Maitland, 1ˢᵗ Earl of Lauderdale.

Once married, Colin Ruadh, as befitted his growing importance, built the castle of Brahan, standing high above the wide River Conan. The five-storey castle, with stair turrets at each of its four angles, was surmounted by parapets from which sentries kept constant watch. The family must have been living there by 1621 for Anna, the youngest of two daughters, is believed to have been born there; in all probability, craftsmen were still hammering away at their work.

The young Lord Seaforth, now in his mid-twenties, continued to be much in favour with King James VI & I. His life, then at its pinnacle, seemed blessed with success. In 1629 he returned, most likely by sea, from the court of London to the family castle at Chanonry, which stood near the site of Fortrose Cathedral on the north side of the Moray Firth.

He must have been eager to see his wife and daughters, Jean and Anna, and in particular Alexander, the youngest of his children, his heir and only son. He was met instead by the terrible news that his young son had died of smallpox.

The date of Alexander's death was 3 June 1629. Mercifully Anna, who was only eight, and also it seems her sister, escaped this horrible and so often fatal disease. Portraits of Anna show her with a flawless and lovely skin. Perhaps the two little girls had been taken to Brahan Castle, a good sixteen miles away, when Alexander first developed the symptoms of this very contagious disease.

The death of young children was then so common that parents were often advised by their elders to try not to love them too much. Nonetheless, when the Countess Margaret died less than two years after little Alexander, on 20 February 1631, it was said that she had pined away partly from grief over the death of her son.

She left behind a young husband to care for Jean and Anna, their two little girls. Alexander MacKenzie, author of the history of his clan, names Lady Anna as the eldest, but Alexander, Lord Lindsay, her biographer (writing in 1868), insists most emphatically that she was the younger of the two.

The children lived in the beautiful new castle, looked after by nurses and other servants, who were mostly barefoot Highland girls. The two little sisters, as Lord Lindsay put it, 'passed their days together among their kinsmen of the clans of

Mackenzie and Ross, in familiarity with the lovely scenery of their father's country, speaking the language of the Gael, and free in spirit as the mountain breezes – Highland maidens in their beauty and simplicity.'[2] Like the local children, they ran barefoot in the summer, hitching up their skirts to splash through the mountain burns as they tried to catch darting speckled trout in their hands.

The days shortened. Rain-laden gales of autumn howled down from the hills. Then came the silence of snow lying deep around the castle. Within the stone walls, by the fireside, their nurse told them stories in the Gaelic of long dead heroes, witches and warlocks, enshrined in the superstitions so endemic amongst Highland people. The river was said to be haunted by a kelpie, a water spirit, and at night the harsh cry of herons could seem like a screech of doom.

Sadly, it seems that they did not see much of their father who, although devoted to them, was largely preoccupied in administering his now largely profitable estates. Colin Ruadh, Earl of Seaforth, made rich by his uncle's management of the land his father had acquired by such dubious means, lived in a style befitting the magnate he had now become. The purchase of wine from the Continent was common practice amongst Scottish gentry and Colin shipped in large quantities which he stored in his refurbished castle at Chanonry on the Black Isle, with its access to the North Sea. From there, his visits to the more remote parts of his estates resembled a royal progress. Reaching Islandonain (Elean donan) he would arrive at the island fortress, claimed the constable, with no fewer than 300 and sometimes 500 men and there they 'consumed the remains of the wine and the liquors'.[3]

From such great expeditions how eagerly his two little daughters, left behind in Brahan Castle, must have longed for his return. The first they would have known of it was when messengers, sent in advance from Chanonry, arrived to

7

warn the household of their coming so that all could be prepared. Then, from a high window, as they strained their ears for the drum of many hoof-beats, they must surely have scanned the horizon for the sight of their father's banner, borne before him as he came. One can imagine them running down to meet him, unafraid of the sweating horses with their stamping hooves as he jumped out of the saddle to swing them up into his arms, then clamouring beside him as they went into the house, all excitement to know what the pack horses had brought. There would probably have been swathes of cloth to be made into dresses: velvets and silks and, undoubtedly greeted with less enthusiasm, cheaper materials suitable for everyday wear. Doubtless there would have been some bickering as to what each girl should possess before they again began rummaging for the sweatmeats he usually brought. Sometimes too he would bring toys, dolls with painted faces, wood-carved animals, plaited ropes for skipping, ribbons to wind into their hair. Best of all on such a special occasion they would probably have been allowed to stay up long after their normal bed-time, as they feasted with their father and the gentlemen of his private retinue, his 'fiery tail', sitting close beside him as he sat at the head of the long table within the castle's great hall.

Sadly the world of the two little girls fell apart as their father succumbed to what is described as 'a lingering illness', of which he died, like his son, at Chanonry, on 15 April 1633 aged only thirty-five. Aware that he had not long to live he called the half-brother who was to succeed him, George of Kildene, to his bedside and 'charged him with the protection of his family'[4] but he must have doubted his integrity (rightly, as it turned out – later George was to withhold Anna's dowry), for it is known that he left his youngest daughter to the guardianship of Lord Rothes, his cousin and trusted friend.

It was as well that he did so for, on his death, his daughters were left without a home, the castle, together with the property and the title, passing to George of Kildene. Anna's eldest sister, Lady Jean, who was already betrothed, went to live with the parents of her future husband, the Earl and Countess of Caithness. Anna herself, however, who at this time was only twelve, as already arranged by her father, went instead to the guardianship of his cousin, John Leslie, the 6th Earl of Rothes, in his stronghold of Leslie Castle in Fife.[5]

The Girl Who Grew up in Fyfe

⎯⎯►◆◄⎯⎯

Lady Anna probably travelled by boat from Ross-shire to Fife, or Fyfe as it was often spelled, this being the most common mode of transport for long journeys in Scotland at the time. If so, she would have sailed from Cromarty in one of her uncle's ships, so recently her father's, most likely a brigantine, a two-masted sailing ship rigged square on the foremast and fore and aft with square topsails on the main-mast, or a birlinn, a smaller vessel easier to navigate in coastal waters and much used in the Western Isles. The voyage to Fife in a fair wind would have taken some three to four days. Otherwise, if it was a season of storms, she may have travelled overland, crossing by one of the ferries over the Cromarty Firth and then heading south through mountain passes over the Grampians into Braemar, from thence into Perthshire, from where, ferried across the Tay, she would have at last reached the flatter and more fertile land of Fife. This route, however, seems improbable in view of the fact that it would have required Anna to ride mostly along rough tracks, for a distance of nearly 200 miles. With her baggage strapped onto Highland ponies, and escorted by heavily armed men, she would hardly have been able to cover more than twenty miles a day. Inns where travellers might rest in the Highlands were not only primitive but few, thus the journey by land would have been both long, arduous and dangerous for a girl only twelve years old. Assuming therefore that she came from Ross-shire by sea, Anna probably landed at St Andrews or at one of the other seaports on the Firth of Forth. From there she would have been taken overland to Leslie Castle, her new home.

The old castle, built as a hall-house, of which only the foundations now remain, stood near the present Leslie House, which dates from the eighteenth century, when the need for comfort and elegance had become more important than defence. In the original building, walls which had hitherto been covered with tapestry in a frequently futile attempt to smother the draughts, were by Anna's time covered by linenfold panelling, particularly in the bedrooms. Tables replaced the bare boards, set up at mealtimes on trestles. Curtains hung over windows which replaced the mere slits in the walls, usually covered with hides, which had previously been the only access to both fresh air and light.

These innovations would not have been new to Anna, whose own home, Brahan Castle, built by her father to include such modern ideas, was equally commodious and comfortable. Nonetheless, used as she was to the Highlands, she must have felt lonely and homesick in her new surroundings, where the majority of people spoke only Lowland Scots.

One hopes her young cousins, Lord Rothes' children, were kind to this strange girl whose first language was Gaelic, and who always gazed with such longing to the far distant Highland hills. Lady Margaret, who was a little older than Anna, and John, the Master of Rothes, who was younger, must have shared their lessons with Anna, who, judging by the neat and well-expressed letters which she later sent, became exceptionally literate for a girl of her time.

The 6th Earl of Rothes was a descendant of Sir Norman Leslie, who had acquired a place called Fythkill in Fife. Subsequently the family had continued to extend its influence both in Moray and Fife. George Leslie, 1st Earl of Rothes, had been made a Lord of Parliament, as Lord Leslie of Leven, by King James II of Scotland in 1445.

John Leslie himself is described rather unkindly by John Buchan as a 'heavy-chinned, goggle-eyed, Pickwinian'[1]. Other historians have been more censorious. Professor Gordon Donaldson, calls him 'a man of dissolute life'[2] while Edward Hyde, Lord Clarendon, accuses him of being a hypocrite, 'very free and amorous, and unrestrained in his discourse by any scruples of religion, which he only put on when the parts he had to act required it, and then no man could appear more conscientiously transported'.[3]

Nonetheless, despite these accusations, he seems to have honoured the promise he had made to his dying cousin to look after Anna. Her biographer, Lord Lindsay, calls him good-natured, and there are clear indications that he had a kind side to him, whatever his faults in other ways.

*

Life in Leslie Castle, as in most big houses of the time, followed a prescribed course. There were three main meals. Breakfast consisted largely of fresh bread, baked by the cooks in the special oven built into the wall beside the great kitchen fire. There would also be hot dishes of such things as collops and kidneys, as well as some cold meats. The main meal of the day was dinner, which was usually at about two o'clock, but often postponed until later if, for instance, Lord Rothes had gone hawking or was detained by business in Edinburgh or elsewhere. The last meal was supper, a relatively simple affair, which sometimes consisted of porridge or even bread and milk, although chicken and game birds like grouse and duck, as well as eggs cooked in various ways, were often served up as well.[4]

On fine weekdays, after their lessons, the children went walking or riding in the parks, as fields are known in Scotland even to the present day. The girls always rode side-saddle, usually wearing velvet habits, with long skirts covering their knees, while the boys, in britches, rode astride. Anna is known to have been a fine horsewoman, as later events were to prove.

Sundays were very strictly observed. Lord Rothes marshalled his wife, children and servants to church. They may have had services in the castle, as most great houses at that time contained a chapel, but more probably, at least for the morning service, they went to Markinch kirk.

Anna, wrapped up in a cloak in winter, with her curls tucked under a bonnet – as propriety then demanded – sat in the family pew. Although the sermons were long and often tedious, the kirk itself was seething with a disruption that, at this time, was sweeping through Scotland with ever increasing force.

Aged only twelve, Anna cannot have been actively engaged in the political upheaval which was taking place around her. However, as she grew older, she must have become aware of the comings and goings of men like Alexander Henderson, a minister of the Kirk nearly fanatical in the fervour of his belief, and with the sworn intention to make Presbyterianism the national religion of Scotland.

CHAPTER 3

The Covenanters and the King

Rothes himself was one of the leaders of a group of men of influence who feared that the obdurate devotion of King Charles I to the Episcopalian Church would end in the bishops having ascendancy over Scotland's Privy Council which, since the Reformation in the sixteenth century, had been ruled predominantly by laymen.

Rumour ran wild as to the king's intentions when, in 1634, the number of bishops in the Privy Council was increased to seven. Then a year later the monarch, obsessed with his divine right to rule, showed blatant defiance to the wishes of his Scottish subjects by appointing John Spottiswoode, Archbishop of St Andrews, to succeed the Earl of Kinnoull as Chancellor of the Council, of which Spottiswoode's son was already lord president.[1] The result was anger and confusion; criticism of the king's actions, first murmured, now, in his enforcement of the bishops' rule, exploded into open revolt. Mr Robert Baillie, a moderate Presbyterian, wrote prophetically that 'No man may speak anything in public for the king's part, except he would have himself marked for a sacrifice to be killed one day. I think our people possessed by a bloody devil.'[2]

On 15 November 1635, the leaders of the aggrieved people of Scotland formed themselves into a body of Commissioners, known as the Tables. Four different committees were then formed, consisting of nobles, lairds, burgesses and ministers. Lady Anna's guardian, Lord Rothes, together with his kinsman the Earl of Lindsay, were appointed to the Table of the Nobility, together with the Earl of Loudoun and the young Earl of Montrose.

In January 1636 a new book of canons authorised by royal warrant was published. Extempore prayer was forbidden, although confession was allowed, the king's supreme authority in all church matters being then proclaimed. Most offensive of all, however, was the enforcement of the new liturgy, or prayer book, which appeared in 1637. The king sent his treasurer, the Earl of Traquair, to Scotland with a proclamation enforcing the new liturgy and prohibiting those opposed to it, on pain of treason, from convening again without the consent of the Privy Council.

On 22 February 1638, this infringement of Scottish liberty was read out in Greyfriars kirk in Edinburgh. On that cold day the air was befogged by the breath of the throng of people who packed the church and churchyard to capacity. The excitement was palpable, becoming ever more intense as men struggled with each other, with curses and even blows, to get a better view of the main participants in the drama taking place before their eyes.

Suddenly there was silence as a speaker, who must have climbed to the pulpit or on to a dais in order to be seen and heard, prepared to make an address to those crammed on the floor below. Then shouts of acclaim rose to a crescendo as the black-robed figure of Archibald Johnston of Warriston, a young man of twenty-seven, was recognised as he began to make a public protest against the king's decree. The fifteen-year-old Earl of Montrose climbed on to a barrel to see what was happening and to hear what Warriston, known to be a near religious maniac who would regularly spend fourteen hours in prayer, was about to say in answer to the king's decree.

'James, you will never be at rest till you are lifted up above the rest in three fathoms of rope', foretold Lord Rothes, standing beside him as one of the Table of Nobility.[3]

The upshot of the protest was that Archibald Johnston and Alexander Henderson, a notable scholar, drafted a new version of the old Covenant of 1581, which had denounced popery, adding a few objections of their own.

The Covenant of 1638 pledged those who signed it to 'defend their religion against all innovations not sanctioned by Parliament and Assembly'.[4] In addition it decreed, most importantly, that they must 'stand to the defence of our dread sovereign the King's Majesty, his person and authority, in the defence and preservation of the foresaid true religion, liberties, and laws of this Kingdom [so that] religion and righteousness may flourish, to the glory of God, the honour of the king, and the peace and comfort of us all'.

The Covenant, far from being treacherous, was thus a firm assertion of loyalty to King Charles I. Montrose was one of the first to sign it, on the instigation of Lord Rothes, who also added his name.

*

In 1638 the king made the Marquess of Hamilton his special commissioner in Scotland to deal with the Covenanters. The city of Edinburgh was alive with excitement and speculation as Hamilton arrived in Edinburgh on 7 June bearing two proclamations. Both assured the Scottish people that the canons and the service book would not be forced upon them 'except in such a fair and legal way as should satisfy all our loving subjects'.[5]

One copy ordered that the Covenant should be abolished. The other did not. Hamilton was told to assess the situation before making his own decision as to which of the documents should be publicly proclaimed.

In Edinburgh he met open hostility and distrust. Traquair had already warned him that a demand to give up the Covenant would be fatal to any form of negotiation with its adherents. However, it was Rothes who, with his innate knowledge of the aims and beliefs of the Covenanters, particularly in regard to their loathing of episcopacy, was generally accepted as the man most conversant with their cause.

For this reason Hamilton, uncertain now as to how to proceed, turned to Lord Rothes for advice. Their discussion led to the formation, by the Tables, of a committee consisting of three churchmen and three nobles, one of whom was Montrose. The Committee of the Tables then asked specifically for the removal of both the canons and the service book before demanding a free General Assembly which would make its own rules. Following this they asked for the summoning of a Scottish parliament, which would legalise the decisions of the Assembly, with the king's consent.

Hamilton then returned to England to find the king as obdurate as ever on the subject of the Covenant, which, he insisted, must be withdrawn. Instead he proposed a Covenant of his own. The Catholic religion would be outlawed but episcopacy, the rule of the Church by bishops, must remain. Pressed by Hamilton, at the instigation of the Covenanters, who wished for a demonstration of good will, he agreed with much reluctance to the calling of a General Assembly, although in his own mind he had already decided to use the arbitration of war.

Unaware of King Charles's intentions, the Covenanters determined to pack the Assembly to try to achieve their aims. It was quickly decided that 'the ablest and best affected gentlemen in ilk paroch be put on the kirk session so that they may be in optione to the commissioners from the presbyteries'. The result was that the 'elders' at the Assembly comprised seventeen peers, nine knights, twenty-five lairds and forty-seven representatives from the burghs, ninety-eight men in all. 'Not a gown was among them all, but many had swords and daggers about them'.[6]

As the king's representative, Hamilton challenged the elders, protesting that laymen had been elected in an unlawful way. 'You have called for a free General Assembly . . . let God and the world judge whether the least shadow or footstep of freedom can be discerned in this assembly.'[7] Hamilton, in high dudgeon, then dissolved the meeting. Rothes protested and Alexander Henderson refused to accept the dissolution. Subsequently the Earl of Argyll, who had only just joined the Covenanters, presided as Privy Councillor over the Assembly, which continued until 20 December.

In England King Charles was raising an army with which he hoped to subdue the Covenanters by force. The Scottish rebels, as he termed them, were also preparing to fight for their religion with the help of one of the ablest and most experienced generals of their day: the mercenary soldier Alexander Leslie.* In the words of the historian, Spalding, 'there came out of Germany hame to Scotland ane gentleman of base birth born in Balveny, who had served long and fortunately in the German wars, and called to his name Felt Marshall Leslie, His Excellence'.[8]

Returning to Scotland on the summons of the Tables, the burden of command of the Army of the Covenant fell on the fifty-six-year-old 'little crooked soldier' during what came to be known as the Bishops' Wars.[9] Once back in Scotland the little general, with his pointed beard and hair falling to his shoulders, became a frequent visitor to Leslie Castle. Lord Rothes welcomed him, both as a distant relation and as the

---

* Alexander Leslie, who is thought to have been born in 1582, was probably the son of George Leslie of Balgonie, who had commanded the garrison of the castle of Blair in the reign of James V. On becoming a mercenary soldier he had gone first to Holland and then to Sweden where, under the patronage of the warlike King Gustavus Adolphus, he had risen to become a Field Marshal.

father-in-law of his daughter, Lady Margaret, who had married Leslie's son, also called Alexander, in 1636, some two years before the general's return.[10]

By 1 May 1639 the Marquis of Hamilton had arrived in the Firth of Forth, almost in sight of Leslie Castle, causing fear almost amounting to panic with nineteen ships of war carrying no fewer than five thousand soldiers. Rothes' immediate reaction was to call out his fencible men (those between sixteen and sixty who were fit enough to fight). His neighbours did likewise and Hamilton, confronted with such unexpectedly strong opposition, lost his nerve. Abandoning the idea of a mainland landing, he ordered his ships back to sea to make ineffectual attacks on the islands in the Firth of Forth.

Word then reached Edinburgh that the king, who had reached York, had proclaimed that he would not allow the Scots to invade England and that he did not propose to invade Scotland 'if all civil and temporal obedience was shown to him'.[11] This was supposed to offer conciliation to the Covenanters but a price of £500 was put upon their general's head. Leslie, thus affronted, then wasted no time in marshalling the Scottish army on the links of Leith, from where he marched to the Border by way of Dunglass.

Negotiations followed at which the chief arbiters for the Scots, who spoke with the king himself, were Lord Rothes, Johnston of Warriston and Alexander Henderson. Thanks to their straight-talking the king agreed, with great reluctance, that the General Assemblies should deal with ecclesiastical matters and parliament with civil issues. A free General Assembly and a free parliament having been convened for the ensuing month of August, the opposing armies were disbanded and subsequently a treaty called the Pacification of Berwick was signed on 19 June 1639.

*

But the Scots did not disarm. Neither did the king come to the parliament or the General Assembly. Instead, on 20 August, the Army of the Covenant crossed the Tweed into England. General Leslie then continued, almost unopposed, to the Tyne ford of Newburn, four miles north of Newcastle. On 28 August, he won a decisive victory over the Royalist army. Then, as the town surrendered, he occupied Newcastle on 30 August.

Subsequently, on 14 October, the Treaty of Ripon was signed, by which the Covenanters agreed to occupy the six northern counties of England for which service they would be paid £850 a day.

Charles was then forced to summon 'The Short Parliament' as it has since been called, which drafted the terms of the peace settlement by which the king was required to agree to the legislation of the Scots and to withdraw his garrisons from Berwick and Carlisle. Most importantly, consultations were to take place on the reform of the Church of England to Presbyterianism and the Scots were to receive no less than the then-staggering sum of £300,000 before they would return home.

The army of the Covenant was triumphant. It held pre-dominance over the king, who by continuing to misunderstand the disastrous nature of his policies was now sliding, as if propelled by an avalanche towards inevitable ruin.

CHAPTER 4

The Bride of the Master of Balcarres

And what had become of Lady Anna during all this time of national turmoil?

At the time of the signing of the Covenant in Greyfriars kirk, she was only just seventeen. Young as she was, she must have been aware of the clandestine meetings at Leslie Castle and of the great involvement of her guardian, Lord Rothes, in the struggle between the king and the Covenanters that was then taking place. A letter that Rothes was shortly to write to Anna indicates that, while under his roof, he had come to regard her almost as a child of his own. He seems genuinely to have regretted that his responsibility towards her would perforce come to an end when she married. That this was shortly to happen soon became obvious. A portrait of Anna, painted at about the time of her marriage, shows her as a strikingly beautiful young woman, with large, wide-apart brown eyes, a fair skin and glorious auburn ringlets.

Furthermore, in addition to her striking looks, she was also, as her father's heiress, an exceedingly desirable match. Lord Rothes, however he deterred her suitors, found himself defeated by the perseverance of a young man who was none other than her own first cousin, Alexander, Master of Balcarres.

Alexander was the son of Anna's aunt, Sophia, a daughter of the Earl of Dunfermline – he who, as Chancellor of Scotland, had supported Lady Anna's grandfather, Kenneth, Lord Kintail, and engineered his escape from Edinburgh Castle.

Born in 1618, Alexander Lindsay was three years older than Anna and, having just returned from a tour of the Continent, was now at St Andrews University, from where he returned to Balcarres Castle during the holidays. A portrait by the artist Jamesone shows him to have been handsome, with fair skin and auburn hair worn loose onto his shoulders, as was the fashion at the time. To Anna, who had never left Scotland, he must have seemed very sophisticated while he, for his part, fell instantly in love with her, by all accounts an intelligent and very lovely girl.

Correspondence in the Lindsay family archives proves that Anna's father, doubting the integrity of his half-brother George, had acted most wisely in placing her under the guardianship of his cousin, Rothes. George, 2nd Earl of Seaforth, was exceedingly angry that, as Lord Lindsay puts it, 'he obtained no feudal or family alliance' through the match. It turns out that some time previously, he had paid a visit to Leslie Castle, where he had noticed that the charming young Master of Balcarres was a very frequent visitor, riding over to Leslie from his father's castle nearby.

Seaforth, guessing the reason, had ordered his niece to come home with him to Ross-shire but had met with a sharp rebuff when Anna told him bluntly that her cousin the Master had 'made love to her' or, in the phraseology of those days, courted her. Seaforth, absolutely furious that a girl of her age should defy him, let alone make her intentions clear, had then threatened to rob her of her inheritance, claiming to have the right to do so. He went off to find John, Lord Lindsay of the Byres, a kinsman of both Anna and himself, to ask him to back his cause. In fact he was wasting his time, for the Master of Balcarres promptly declared that he wanted no money and that he would marry Lady Anna entirely 'for her own sweet self'.[1]

John Lindsay of the Byres, when told of this, immediately came in on the side of the young couple, as did other relations, who included their first cousin, the young Earl of Dunfermline, and also Lord Wintoun.

Meanwhile Seaforth, who had retired in high dudgeon to the Highlands, was mollified to some extent by a letter from the Master of Balcarres himself.

Alexander wrote to him from Edinburgh, on 18 January 1640:

My Lord,

If I had known you had been to go out of this country so soon as you did, I would have spoken to your Lordship that which I am forced to write: for I can forbear no longer to tell your Lordship of my affection to your niece, and to be an earnest suitor to your Lordship for your consent to that wherein only I can think myself happy. The Earl of Rothes and my Lord Lindsay have shown me how averse your Lordship was from it, and in truth I was very sorry for it. They have both laboured, more than I desired them, to divert me from it as a thing which would never have your Lordship's approbation, without which she could not have that portion which her father left her; but I protest to your Lordship, as I have done to them, that my affection leads me beyond any consideration of that kind, for (God knows) it was not her means which made me intend it – and therefore my Lord, since both by the law of God and man marriage should be free, and that she who it concerns most nearly is pleased to think me worthy of her love, I am confident that your Lordship, who is stead of a father to her, will not continue in your averseness from it, but even look to that which she, who has greatest interest, thinks to be for her weal; for none but one's self can be judge of their own happiness.

If it shall seem good to your Lordship to give me that favourable answer which I expect from your hands, since (as

I hear) your Lordship is not to be in this country shortly, I
hope ye will be pleased to entrust some of your friends here
who may meet about the business with my father; and I
believe your Lordship will get all just satisfaction in the
conditions. I hope your Lordship will never have cause to
repent of your consent to this; for, though you get no great
new allys, yet your Lordship will keep that which you have
had before, and gain one who is extreme desirous, and shall
on all occasions be most willing to be

Your Lordship's most humble servant,

A Lyndesay

At Edinbruch, 18 Jan, 1640[2]

Seaforth, on receiving this, reluctantly gave his consent to
Alexander's marriage to his niece. Whereupon Alexander
wrote to him again:

I should think myself very unworthy if I were not more
careful nor anybody else that she be well provided. I know
my father will do all he can, and I hope your Lordship and
all the rest of her friends shall see my care in this hereafter.[3]

Lady Anna MacKenzie and Alexander Lindsay, Master of
Balcarres, were married in April 1640. The wedding probably
took place in the bride's adoptive home, Leslie Castle, as was
the custom in those days. Anna would most likely have worn a
dress of silk or satin trimmed at the bodice and on the sleeves
with lace or a similar material. Also, for her wedding she would
have worn family jewels, which, pearls being then the height of
fashion, may well have included the necklace and the cross
emblazoned with pearls and diamonds that are shown in her
portrait, believed to have been painted at about this time. In
this she wears a pale blue dress; a snood of what seems to be
crimson velvet, interlaced with diamonds, is fastened upon the

back of her head, holding in place the auburn ringlets which fall to her shoulders below her milk-white throat.

The ceremony over, the wedding breakfast would have commenced with jollity with family and friends. Then, probably after their first night together as man and wife, the young couple would have set off for Balcarres Castle to the cries of fond farewells. Presumably they travelled in Lord Balcarres' family coach unless, being young, they chose to ride, eastwards from Leslie Castle, to Balcarres Castle, in Fife.

*

In Fife in April, the grass would just have been beginning to appear. Once summer came, however, each farm would have a field blue with the flowers of the flax, which, brought in from the Low Countries, had been found to grow so well. Every farmhouse had its spinning wheel on which the coarse fibers, prised from the stalks, were spun to be woven into cloth.

The stone-built farmhouses, with the cottar's dwellings surrounding them, were thatched with straw. Outside them ducks and hens scrambled over middens, while the cattle, which had been housed in the winter, were newly turned out to graze.

The real wealth of Fife, however, lay in its coalmines, to which men were indentured for life. Much of the coal was used to fire the saltpans that proliferated along the coast. At high tide, seawater poured through man-made channels into a pond. It was then carried in buckets to the saltpans, from which the water evaporated as fires burnt beneath them. Smoke rose into the air from every sea-girt village. It was thanks to the coal, the salt, the crops that grew so well on the good arable land, and the animals that it raised that the Lindsays of Balcarres, at the time of Anna's marriage, were one of the most influential and prosperous families in the east of Scotland.

From the coast the landmark of the Craig of Balcarres is visible, a rocky height, since partly quarried, and in those days bare of trees. Below was the family chapel and beyond, surrounded by its parks, the old castle of Balcarres, the stone gleaming with brightness in the clear light of spring. This would be Alexander's inheritance, handed down through a line of men who in the course of their lifetimes had achieved both substance and fame.

The Lindsays, who by the time of the Norman Conquest were holding large territories in both England and Scotland, had prospered through attaining high office under the rule of successive Scottish kings. On St Georges's Day, 23 April 1390, David, Lord Crawford, representing the chivalry of Scotland, had fought a passage of arms with Lord Welles on London Bridge before King Richard II and his queen, Anne of Bohemia, 'when he displayed great prowess and unhorsed his antagonist'.[4] Married to the daughter of King Robert II of Scotland, he was subsequently created Earl of Crawford and became Admiral of Scotland and Ambassador to England in 1406, the year when, during the reign of Henry IV, the young King James I of Scotland, captured by pirates at sea, was taken prisoner to England.

The Lindsays of Balcarres were descendants of John Lindsay, Lord Menmuir, second son of the 9th Earl of Crawford, whose son, David Lindsay, was created Lord Lindsay of Balcarres by King Charles I in 1633. This was the man who, together with his wife Lady Sophia (Anna's aunt) on that April day, was waiting to welcome their son and new young daughter-in-law to Balcarres.Their eldest daughter, also called Sophia, only two years younger than Anna herself, was also there to meet them, as were the members of the castle staff, all eager to see the young bride of whose beauty so much had been told.

Anna's new home was more modern than that which she

had just left, the Z-plan tower house having been built in 1595, not yet fifty years earlier. Some fine oak panelling, carving and plasterwork of the original castle remain in Balcarres Castle today. The property had belonged to the Lindsay lords of Menmuir since 1587, some twelve years before the castle was built. Now the lands of Wester Pitcorthie and Balmakin and Balbuthie, dependencies of the barony of Balcarres, were assigned to Lady Anna as her jointure, together with the 'East Lodging' and adjacent buildings on the east side of the castle courtyard, on both sides of the east gate, which part of the castle was to become the 'Dower House' for generations to come.

Lord Lindsay, whose biography of Anna was published in 1868, here writing largely from hearsay, gives a charming account of Balcarres as it was when she first went there as a bride:

> The old house at Balcarres [had a] paved cloister or court . . . towers, turrets, and gabled roofs without, and . . . deeply recessed window seats, curiously stuccoed ceilings, and winding turnpike stair within . . . Hollies and ilexes, and loftier elms, and other forest trees, planted by David Lord Balcarres and by his father Secretary Lindsay, [most of them, in Lindsay's day] still surviving and the home of thousands of rooks, surrounded the house.[5]

Back at Leslie Castle Anna was so missed that one guesses Lord and Lady Rothes may have spoiled the sad little orphaned girl from the Highlands to whom they had given a home for seven years. This much is indicated from the letter which Lord Rothes, her guardian, wrote to her, about three weeks after the day when she had left Leslie Castle. Plainly he had been doing his annual accounts! Perhaps she had overspent on clothes for her wedding and, from what he says, she may have been gambling at cards, at that time a passion with the aristocracy, men and women alike. He also seems to have realised that with her beauty and charm, she could twist both her husband and her new in-laws round the fingers of her small white hands. Rothes writes as a guardian who still feels responsible for her welfare and behaviour even after she has left his care. His term of endearment, which indicates great affection, is not unusual, it being a commonplace greeting at that time:

My heart,

I have sent Mr David Ayton with your compts since my intromission; they are very clear and well instructed, but truly your expence hath been over large this last year, it will be about 3,600 merks, which indeed did discontent me when I looked on it. I hope ye will mend it in time coming; and give me leave, as bound both by obligation and affection, to remember you that you must accommodate yourself to that estate whereof you are to be mistress, and be rather an example of parsimony nor a mover of it in that family. Your husband hath a very noble heart, and much larger than his fortune, and except you be both an example and an exhorter of him to be sparing, he will go over far . . . he [and] my Lord and Lady, love you so weill that if ye incline to have those things that will beget expence, they will not be wanting although it will do them harm, they being all of a right noble disposition; therefore a sparing disposition and practice on your part will not only benefit you in so far as it concerns your own personal expence, but it will make your husband's expence, and your good-sister's [sister-in-law] the less also; for, your and their expence being all to come out of one purse, what is spent will spend on you, and what is spared is to your behoof, for I hope your good-father and good-mother will turn all they have to the behoof of your husband

and you, except the provision for their other children, and
the more will be spared that your personal expences be little
– therefore go very plain in your clothes, and play very little,
and seek God heartily, who can alone make your life
contented here, and give you that chief content, the hope
of happiness hereafter. The Lord bless you!
   I am your faithful friend and servant,
   Rothes[6]

Lord Rothes' concern about Lady Anna's extravagance and
willfulness is revealed in another letter which he wrote to her
husband at the time. He warns Alexander to check his accounts
as to his expenditure, she being 'a little wilful in the way of her
expences, and my wife could not weill look to her, being
infirm',[7] an indication that with Lady Rothes an invalid, Anna
had seized the chance to order clothes and jewellery which
Lord Rothes had then had to pay for. Unwilling to besmirch
her character however, he then adds optimistically 'I hope in
God she shall prove ane good wise woman, and sparing
eneuch. And you must even conform yourself to your estate'.[8]
   All of this, to Alexander, was like water off a duck's back. He
adored his young wife, as did his parents, his father writing
shortly afterwards of 'her mild nature and sweet disposition, wise
withal'. This must have been one of the last letters which David,
Lord Balcarres was to write, for he died the following March,
in1641. His wife's brother-in-law, John Maitland, Lord Lauderdale (who had married Isabel, third daughter of the Earl of
Dunfermline), then at Whitehall, wrote a letter of condolence to
his nephew Alexander, now Lord Balcarres, telling him that:

The death of my noble lord, your father, I may justly say,
was as grievous to me as to any other soever next to my sister
and her children, not only for the loss which I perceive now,
and will feel more sensibly when it shall please God to bring

me home, of so worthy and kind a brother, but even for the want which the public will sustain of one of so great worth, whose service might have been so useful both to King and State. But one thing doth comfort us all, who had so near interest in him, that it has pleased God to bless him with a son of such abilities as God has endued your Lordship with; who I am confident shall succeed no less to his virtues than to his inheritance, so that it may be truly said, 'Mortuus est pater, sed quasi non mortuus, quia filium similem reliquit sibi' . . .

Your most affectionate uncle and servant,
Lauderdale.[9]

Alexander's mother, now the Dowager Lady Balcarres, together with her eldest daughter, Sophia, must have moved into the Dower House, in the East Lodging, which, although it was part of Anna's jointure, was what her late husband had intended.

Anna, in place of her mother-in-law, was now the mistress of the castle, a formidable task for a young woman of only just twenty-one. Nonetheless, as in similar cases, she would probably have had a major-domo, who, in all likelihood having served the family for years, was now in a managerial position. The indoor staff, as in most large houses of the time, were in fact mostly male, the fetching and carrying of water for all household uses, and of wood and coal for the kitchen, besides the fires in almost every room throughout the house, requiring physical strength. The women worked as cooks, scullery maids, laundry maids and housemaids, the latter of whom, on hands and knees, had to scrub both wooden and stone floors and flights of spiral stairs. A maid in charge of the still-room made jams and jellies, items such as candles with both tallow and wax, beeswax for polishing and dried rose petals for the pot pourri which so sweetly scented the rooms.

Also, most importantly, she pounded roots, dried herbs and spices into powder for the medicines which, with all the other contents, filled the shelves on the walls.

Wine and brandy imported from abroad, mainly from Flanders and France, were kept locked in a well-stocked cellar. However ale, made at home by a brewster, was the staple drink of most households, tea then being a luxury imported at great expense.

Anna, at least at the start of her marriage, with all her new responsibilities in running a large household, could rely on the support of her husband. In addition, the Reverend Mr Forret, like a benevolent shadow, could always be turned to for advice. Meeting him, on her arrival at Balcarres, she can hardly have guessed at the part the good clergyman was to play in their future lives. As her husband's private tutor first at home, then at the grammar school at Haddington and finally at St Andrews University, he had influenced Alexander's adolescent years to the point of becoming almost a second father. Shortly, on the incumbent of Kilconquhar either dying or retiring, Alexander was to offer him the living of the parish, in which, as the records prove, he remained until very old age. Meanwhile, his association with the family continued to be so close that he shared their joys and sorrows as his own.

In addition to overseeing her household, Anna became a passionate gardener. She planted all sorts of flowers, including what Lord Lindsay wrote 'would nowadays be accounted weeds'. Some of the seeds came from abroad, as did the Bergamot pears which Sir Robert Moray, Alexander's closest friend and then in the service of Cardinal de Richelieu, sent over from Paris. Surprisingly they did well on the walls of Balcarres, one presumes in a walled garden, 'notwithstanding the exposed climate of the east of Fifeshire'. Anna, with Alexander, planted a grove which old people still called the 'New Plantation' in Lord Lindsay's own time.[10]

Notable as he was both for his great interest in cultivation and in the agricultural improvements which were by then being introduced to Scotland, Alexander Lindsay was also recognised as one of the leading thinkers and academics of his day. Balcarres Castle housed a library full of rare books, collected originally by his father and grandfather, but much added to by himself. Here he and his cousin, John Lauderdale (who succeeded his father as second earl in 1645), spent many happy hours in what Lord Lindsay calls 'bibliomaniacal councel' with Lady Anna acting as intermediary when the arguments between them became too excited and involved.[11]

CHAPTER 5

The Civil War

Following his defeat by the Scottish army, the king, now in desperate need of a man he could trust, turned to Thomas Wentworth, whom he had created Earl of Strafford and Lord Lieutenant of Ireland. Strafford coerced the Irish parliament into granting funds for the king to raise a new army with which to fight the Scots. However, before these reinforcements could arrive, the king's army had been defeated by the army of the Covenanters under General Leslie's command.

Funds for the army came from tax and, then as now, all taxes had to be approved by parliament. The king had summarily dismissed the Short Parliament in May 1640, but by November his need for money to support the Scottish army of occupation in Northumberland and Durham forced him to call parliament again. This session was not so easily dismissed, and became known as the Long Parliament (although closed by Cromwell in 1653, it was only finally dissolved in 1660). King Charles was now forced into a position where his great need for funds placed him largely in the power of men who, in defiance of his own belief in his divine right to rule, were determined to limit his power.

One of the first actions of the Long Parliament, headed by the Puritan John Pym, was to demand the impeachment of Strafford on the grounds that he had treasonably urged the king to use the Irish army against his foes in England as well as against the Scots. The case against him was unproven, but when Strafford's opponents acquired a bill of attainder (a conviction for an act of treason), the king, in an agony of mind, agreed to his execution on 12 May 1641.

*

The quarrel between King Charles and his parliament was to uproot and in many cases destroy the hitherto largely peaceful existence of families throughout both England and Scotland. The young Lord and Lady Balcarres were no exception, for at this time both Countess Anna, as she had become, and her husband, perhaps to some extent influenced by family connections, were devoted to the cause of the Covenant.

Yet despite their growing anxiety over what now seemed to most people in Scotland to be impending war, Anna and Alexander had a brief time of happiness when, in the early summer of 1641, their first child, the heir to Balcarres, was born. David Lindsay was baptised by the Reverend Mr Forret, at Kilconquhar, on 3 June. Sadly his parents' joy dissolved into heartrending grief as their little boy died as an infant, of what cause we do not know. Anna herself, who was only twenty, must then have thought much of her mother, that shadowy figure who had died when Anna was only two. She too had lost her first-born son, and grief was thought to have hastened her death. Now, consoled by the wise Mr Forret, Anna tried to find comfort in the belief that her child was in the arms of Christ. Fortunately she soon became pregnant again and a daughter, Anne, was born in the autumn of the following year. She was baptised at Kilconquhar on 16 November 1642.

Meanwhile, in this short interlude of peace, both Alexander Balcarres and his wife enjoyed the peaceful surroundings of their lovely home. But, like everyone in Scotland and England who was aware of events in London, they realised all too quickly that the quarrel between the king and his parliament in

England and the Privy Council in Scotland, now dominated by the Earl of Argyll, must result in renewed warfare unless, by some miracle, agreement between the parties could be reached.

*

King Charles was in Scotland from mid-August until mid-November in 1641. During the first two weeks he reached a good understanding with Rothes, who by now mistrusted Argyll (whom the king had just made a marquess), believing him to be using the cause of the Covenant to increase his own political power. Rothes did his best to convince the chancellor, the Earl of Loudoun (also a Campbell), of the chief of his clan's duplicity. The Marquess of Hamilton, however, believing any form of reconciliation between the Covenanters and the king to be now impossible, joined forces with Argyll.

Then at the end of August, suddenly and unexpectedly at the age of only forty-one, which even in those days of short life expectancy was considered to be young, Rothes died. His death, coming so soon after that of her baby boy, was an added tragedy for Anna, to whom he had been a father figure for the seven years prior to her marriage since her own parents had died. Likewise for the king, who was still in Scotland at the time, it was a personal disaster in that he now found himself bereft of the one man who, despite his loyalty to the Covenant, kept some control over the extremists who aimed to disrupt his power.

King Charles left Edinburgh on 18 November. Reaching London only to be confronted by angry members of his English parliament, he refused to countenance their Grand Remonstrance, which demanded a government presided over by parliament and a meeting of bishops to define the policy of the Anglican Church. Having tried and failed to arrest five members of the House of Commons, he left London to begin raising an army. The Parliamentarians did likewise, and in August 1642 the Civil War in England began.

Four months later appeals were made to the Scottish parliament by both the English government and the king. Subsequently, in the spring of 1643, Chancellor Loudoun and the Presbyterian minister, Alexander Henderson, went to Charles in Oxford and told him bluntly that the Scottish Council would agree not to support the English Parliamentarians only on his specific assurance that he would reform the Church of England to Presbyterian rules. Predictably, the king refused to comply with what to him was a perfectly outrageous demand. The Parliamentarians sent commissioners to Scotland to ask for an alliance which would include not only military support, but the continuance of the supply of Scottish coal to London. They arrived on 7 August to find that the General Assembly had already been convened five days earlier.

On 17 August another declaration, this time called the Solemn League and Covenant, was drawn up, detailing the preservation of the reformed church in Scotland, the reformation of religion in England and Ireland, and the subsequent unity of the three churches involved. The English government, having accepted the Solemn League, then organised an agreement with the Scottish Council by which 18,000 foot soldiers and 2,000 cavalry were to be sent to England to fight against the king.

To James Graham, the young Earl of Montrose, this amounted to treachery. The king, so he reasoned, had given the Scots all they wanted. Now, in siding with his enemies, they were submitting to the aggrandisement of a faction of their leaders led by the man whom Rothes had mistrusted, the Marquess of Argyll. Montrose rode to Oxford in February 1643 and put his case to the king, assuring him that in Scotland his cause might yet be saved. Charles would not listen to him at first, preferring to put his trust in Hamilton at the instigation of his French queen, the Catholic Henrietta Maria. Then, becoming aware at last that Hamilton, as a negotiator, was both untrustworthy and ineffective, he made Montrose both a marquess and lieutenant-general of his army in Scotland.

Meanwhile, in Scotland, the fencible men were again summoned to arms. At Balcarres, as her husband struggled to find enough money to buy horses and to arm and equip his local men, Countess Anna sold some of her jewels. Both of them, at this point, seem still to have believed in the integrity of the political leaders of the Covenant, of which their uncle, Lord Lauderdale, President of the Scottish Parliament, was now in increasing doubt. When Lauderdale died, while still president of the Scottish Parliament, on 18 January 1645, it was said he had succumbed from despair over the state of Scotland more than from any physical illness.

*

On 19 January 1644, in freezing weather, the army of the Covenant, commanded by General Alexander Leslie, crossed the border into England. Balcarres went with him, leading a company of his own men. This was the foundation of the regiment, later described with some pride by Lord Alexander Lindsay as 'the strongest force in the kingdom'.[1] Eventually the cost of the provisions and equipment of so large a company of men was to become so exorbitant that, like so many others in similar circumstances, Balcarres would be forced to sell his family's plate (which was made of gold or possibly of silver).

The summons to arms was sent out by runners carrying the fiery cross, the charred piece of lime wood which, from time immemorial, had been recognised as a call to arms. Most of Balcarres' soldiers were his own tenants, who, with their hardy ploughmen, dressed in their homespun jackets and trews, rode or walked to Balcarres Castle. There, after entering the courtyard, they were summoned into the great hall to be equipped with the guns, swords and pikes, taken out of the armoury and sharpened by blacksmiths, after a period of little use. The noise of their gathering would have been near-deafening, horses neighing, men shouting and the constant thudding of many feet up and down the castle's stone stairs.

One can picture Countess Anna, pregnant at the time, climbing up the steps of the spiral staircase, her long skirts rustling on the stone as she went up to the battlements to see her husband ride away at the head of his regiment of horse. Her eyes must have followed his banner dwindling into the distance, the noise gradually lessening as the newly made soldiers and the supply wagons which followed them slowly moved out of sight. Watching with pride, she probably stifled her fear in the knowledge that he was fighting for his country and his Church. Then she was left in a castle inhabited only by women and a few retainers too ancient to fight, where, as the men left them, silence fell over the walls.

*

Anna was certainly both lonely and anxious as she waited for news of her husband, whom, as the weeks passed, she guessed to be in the north of England. The days may have seemed to pass slowly despite the fact that, under the circumstances, she was probably occupied almost from dawn until dusk.

As has always been customary in times of war the women left at home, in many instances, had to carry out the tasks of men. It was now that Anna first displayed the competence for which she became so justly famed. Life at that time, in Scotland as elsewhere, depended on the produce of the land. Anna, although not involved in manual work, may well have had to buy such necessary items as seed corn and later oversee the storage in the cellars of the grain and salted carcasses on which, until the following harvest, her own family and those of all their retainers would survive.

*

Seven months had passed since Alexander Balcarres had ridden across the border into England on that ice-cold January day. Rumours of what was happening, and almost certainly letters, had reached Anna but it was not until late summer, as hay was being cut and stacked, that she heard news of the great battle in which her husband had first fought.

It had begun on 2 July when the king's nephew, Prince Rupert of the Rhine, had launched an attack against the combined armies of the Covenant and the Parliamentarians on the stretch of ground near York known as Marston Moor.

In the first stages of the conflict the two armies faced each other across a ditch hedged in on either side. The Royalists, however, had the best position, being placed on the open moor, while the Parliamentarians were on uneven ground, partly hemmed in by hedges and bushes of gorse and whin. Oliver Cromwell, with about 3,000 cavalry of the Eastern Association, was on the left wing. Sir Thomas Fairfax, with about 2,000 of the Northern cavalry, was on the right.

The infantry of both the Scottish Army, commanded by the Earl of Leven, and the English, under Lord Fairfax, were massed in the centre. The musketeers and pikemen, wearing iron corselets and headpieces, carried both pike and sword to repel a cavalry charge. The cavalry of the Scottish army had been divided to form a reserve, about 800 mounted soldiers being behind the English on each wing. General David Leslie, grandson of Lord Rothes, had asked to go with Cromwell for, as he said, 'Europe has no better cavalry'.[2]

David Leslie spoke from experience. Having served in the army of Gustavus Adolphus, he had learned the strategy of the man renowned across Europe as an expert in the art of war. Cromwell, equally aware of Gustavus Adolphus' expertise, had drilled his own Model Army in the tactics of the Swedish king. It was now generally accepted that an efficient army needed a cavalry at least half the size of the infantry. The old heavy cavalry was largely replaced by arquebusiers, armed with sword, pistol and carbine, and with dragoons wearing a light steel casque, a cuirass or sometimes even a padded leather coat, which could turn the point of a sword.

Once in action they followed the model set by Gustavus, riding knee-to-knee in three-deep formation. Packed tight together, the horses could be guided by the pressure of the leg, leaving their riders' hands free to handle weapons. First advancing at the trot, the horsemen held their fire until within close range of the enemy, charging at full gallop into the opposing front line.

On the Royalist side Prince Rupert, himself acknowledged as a master in the skills of cavalry attack, specifically targeted Cromwell in what amounted to a duel of expertise. Two of the greatest soldiers in Europe were now about to face each other in a headlong charge – then came a stalemate as each of the two armies waited for the other to attack. At half past seven Prince Rupert gave the order for the men to break for supper, it being, as he thought, too late to begin an action that day. Cromwell, seeing this, knew that his moment had come.

The horses, spurred on by their riders, leapt over the ditch. David Leslie, who had moved to the left of Cromwell, crossed it beyond Rupert's front line. At his order the men raised their muskets and fired a deadly hail of lead into the enemy's flank. Alexander Balcarres, fighting behind him with death-defying bravery, made himself an easy target as he rode full-tilt ahead of his men.

Then Cromwell fell, pitched from his saddle by a blow on the back of his neck. Those closest to him wavered, believing him dead, but the Scottish soldiers dashed past them, driving the best-trained men of the Royalist army over the sloping ground, now slippery with blood. Stunned by their impact the famous cavalry of Prince Rupert's army scattered and fled through the dusk towards the city of York.

The Parliamentarians took Newcastle on 19 October and Tynemouth on 27 October. Leven had by then returned to Scotland and his army was in winter quarters. In November Argyll handed in his commission as general-in-chief to the Committee of the Estates, who appointed William Baillie of Letham, one of the best and most experienced of Leven's generals, in his place.[3]

*

While the army of the Covenant had cost the king the north, Montrose had not been inactive. From Blair Atholl he pursued Argyll to his castle of Inveraray where, while Argyll himself escaped in a fishing boat, he laid waste to the little town.

Argyll, having summoned his foremost commander, General Campbell of Auchinbreck, from Ireland, vengefully drove the Royalist army north into Lochaber. Montrose had reached Kilcummin when the Gaelic bard, Iain Lom MacDonald, warned him that Argyll was a short way behind him, encamped at the old castle of Inverlochy.

On 2 February 1645 Montrose, with the great MacDonald, Alasdair MacColla, swept down from the mountain range of Ben Nevis to annihilate the army of the Covenant. Iain Lom MacDonald wrote triumphantly of the victory in which his own clan massacred so many of their Campbell foes. His words, translated, run:

I ascended early on the Sunday morning to the
top of the castle of Inverlochy. I saw the whole
affair, and the battle's triumph was with Clan Donald . . .

A tale most joyful to receive of the Campbells
of the wry mouths – every troop of them as they came
having their heads broken under the blows of the swords . . .

John of Moidart of the bright sails that would
sail the ocean on a dark day, there was no tryst-
breaking with you! And joyful to me was the
news of Barbreck* in your power . . .

Alasdair of the sharp biting blades, you promised,
yesterday to destroy them. You put the rout past
the Castle, guiding right well the pursuit.

The Committee of Estates, terrified by the decimation of
Argyll's army, having first ordered General Alexander Leven
to relinquish some of his best infantry to serve under General
Baillie's command, now asked him for cavalry. Amongst those
transferred was Balcarres's regiment of horse. Balcarres himself, a hero since Marston Moor, became Baillie's Master of the
Horse. Baillie's army had also been strengthened by Balcarres'
cousin, Lord Lindsay of the Byres (granted the forfeited earldom of Crawford), who was given command of a new army
north of the River Tay.

In the last week of June Baillie stationed his army at Keith,
on the Deveron. Montrose then led his army southwards into
Strathdon where, on reaching the village, he contrived to
conceal the greater part of his soldiers behind the shoulder
of a rise called Gallows Hill. Baillie reached Alford on 2 July.

---

* Barbreck = Campbell of Barbreck on Loch Awe, later of Ardnamurchan.

The stretch of the Don below the village, in those days before draining, wound its way through bogs, but was fordable in several places. Baillie encamped on marshy ground to the south of the river from where the lowing of Huntly's captured cattle infuriated the Gordons in the Royalists' camp behind the nearby Gallows Hill.

General Baillie was hesitant about advancing but Balcarres, believing that a thin line of men he could see on the top of the hill were retreating, charged, at the head of his regiment, across a ford. Instantly, even as the horses were splashing across, he realised his mistake . . .

In a thunderous roar of hoofbeats, Lord Gordon, with his 250 horsemen, launched a furious onslaught on the left flank of the Covenant army. The foot soldiers were scattered, unable to stand the impetus of bullets and flailing swords. The battle became a contest between the cavalry of both sides. Balcarres, with his three squadrons of horse, fought magnificently, oblivious it seemed to fear, until the Irish soldiers, under the command of Alasdair MacDonald, rushed in and hauched, or ham-strung, his horses with cruel blows from their swords.

Seizing the chance of this slaughter, the Royalists then closed in on the Covenant centre, which, with dreadful casualties, was totally overthrown. Baillie and Balcarres, with the few surviving cavalry who had astonishingly managed to escape, made their way south to Perth. Behind them the unfortunate foot soldiers of the Covenant army were left to die on the field or be hunted down by the merciless Irish contingent of the Royalists as they fled through the length of Strathdon.

Inevitably there was bitter discrimination over such an unpredictable and apparently unwarranted defeat. Balcarres was accused of being precipitous but, as invariably happens, it was the commander-in-chief who was deemed responsible for the disaster which had overtaken his army. In Perth General

Baillie, called to question, resigned his commission. The Committee of Estates, however, having no one competent of high rank to replace him, persuaded him to change his mind but appointed a Committee of War from amongst their own ranks. Argyll was its head and Balcarres a member.

Shortly afterwards scouts galloped in with the news that Montrose was coming up the valley of the Forth towards Stirling. The Committee of War believed that with the town's one bridge across the Forth heavily guarded he would find himself trapped. They were soon to hear, however, that he had forded the river above the town and was heading south for Glasgow across the Carse of Stirling and over the Campsie Fells.

In the full heat of August the army of the Covenant followed the trail of hoof-marks and trodden grass over the Campsie Fells to Kilsyth. On 16 August, just above the village, they caught sight of the enemy entrenched in the outskirts of the village where the hedges and dykes in the outlying fields gave good protection against attack. It was obvious to Baillie and to Balcarres, the only two members of the Committee of War with any real knowledge of military tactics, that the stretch of rough ground immediately before them would impede a cavalry charge. Neither wanted to risk a battle but Argyll and the other members thought otherwise, insisting that by taking a small hill between them and Montrose's position, they would have a tremendous advantage over the men on the lower ground. Baillie and Balcarres were outvoted. The advance began.

It was now so hot that the Highland men and the Irish in Montrose's regiment threw off their heavy woollen plaids, preparing to fight in their long saffron shirts, made of rough linen, as they waited with musket and sword.

The Covenanters moved forward slowly, Balcarres leading his cavalry in front of the foot soldiers, over the rough ground.

Then as some of the musketeers saw a party of MacDonalds creeping towards them through gorse bushes, they opened fire. Their estimate of the range was inaccurate. The bullets fell short and with that the MacDonalds were upon them before they had time to reload. Simultaneously some of the Gordon cavalry attacked another part of the line. The Covenanters broke ranks in confusion and, as he saw this opportunity, Montrose launched a full attack.

Balcarres, trying to rally his horsemen, found it impossible to re-form them before they met the full onslaught of the Royalist cavalry, led by old Lord Airlie, as it crashed into their midst. Around him, in total confusion, men were deserting, running in abject terror from the terrible two-edged battle-axes and claymores which the Highlanders and the Irish used with such deadly accuracy. Balcarres fought on until, seeing the position was hopeless, he withdrew from that field of death with as many of his cavalry soldiers as were still able to sit on their horses.

CHAPTER 6

Commissioners of the Covenant

⸺➤●◀⸺

Montrose then seemed invincible, but less than a month later, on 13 September, he himself only just escaped from an even more terrible slaughter at Philiphaugh, on the River Yarrow, when General David Leslie, taking him by surprise in an early morning mist, nearly destroyed his army in a catastrophic defeat.

This was the Armageddon for the Royalist army in Scotland. Although Montrose himself continued to fight a form of guerrilla warfare in the north-east, the most influential noble in the region, the Earl of Huntly, who had always been jealous, refused to join forces with him. Only Anna's uncle, Lord Seaforth, who had vacillated for many months, now, when it was too late, came to Montrose's support and finally declared for the king.

Meanwhile, in England, Parliament became dominated by the so-called Independents, headed by Oliver Cromwell, Henry Ireton and Sir Thomas Fairfax, commander of the New Model Army. King Charles, whose last major field army had been destroyed at the Battle of Naseby in 1645, knowing that the ultimate aim of the Parliamentarians was to depose him with a view to establishing a republic in England, decided, after much prevarication, to seek support from the Scottish Army of the Covenant.

He did so confident in the assurance of the French ambassador, Montreuil, who had liaised with the leaders of the

Covenant in Scotland, that they would 'receive the king with safety and honour'.¹ Although adamant that he must accept their Presbyterian doctrine, they still professed themselves to be loyal to the crown.

Accordingly, at three o'clock in the morning on 25 April 1646, Charles, with his hair cut short and wearing a false beard, supposedly a servant, rode out from Oxford behind John Ashburnham, one of his Grooms of the Bedchamber and his chaplain, Michael Hudson.

At an inn near Nottingham the three exhausted men appeared at seven in the morning of 5 May. The French ambassador had gone out to look for him, and the king, utterly worn out, lay down on his bed and went to sleep.

The Scottish army was laying siege to Newark, just four miles away to the east. Rumour of the king's escape had by now reached Edinburgh. There the Committee of Estates, without waiting to hear that he had actually reached their army at Newark, at once dispatched Lord Balcarres 'with offers to the King of defence and assistance on the condition that he should recognise and secure their liberties, civil and religious, in terms of the Covenant'.²

Alexander Balcarres must have ridden through day and night, stopping only to change horses and snatch a hasty meal at one of the posting inns before reaching Southwell almost as the king arrived. He found him frail and tired but adamant in his refusal to agree to the proffered terms. The principal Commissioner, the Earl of Lothian, then joined the king at Southwell. He treated the king with studied politeness but met with the same stubborn refusals to the offers of the Covenanters as had Balcarres.

The Covenanters then faced a dilemma as to the fate of the king. The Earl of Lanark (Hamilton's brother), afraid of what was likely to occur, begged him to sign the Covenant. Montreuil added his pleas, urging him to go to Scotland, where at least he might be safe. Argyll told Montreuil that he could not allow the king to come to Scotland, even bound as a prisoner, unless he accepted the Covenant.

On 16 December, in the Scottish parliament, the Estates debated on the vital question of whether the king could be brought into Scotland or not. A vote was taken and, by a large majority, a negative answer was given. Crawford-Lindsay and Balcarres, jumping to their feet, protested vehemently but their voices were drowned in a general hubbub of dissent.[3]

The king himself, when told at Newcastle that Scotland had disowned him, went on quietly playing chess.

On 2 January 1647, the Commissioners from the English parliament arrived at the town. They told the king that he was to be held as a political prisoner, an order with which, having no alternative, he had to comply. On 28 January the Scottish Commissioners came to say farewell. Facing them with quiet dignity, he told them, 'I came to your army at Southwell for your protection and it was granted me.'[4] Shamefaced, they left the room.

Two days later, as the Covenanters, commanded by David Leslie, marched out of Newcastle with drums beating and standards flying, they were pursued by fishwives pelting them with rubbish and yelling 'Judas' to their backs. Behind them they left King Charles, a sad, lonely figure, watching from a window, knowing that he was now to be guarded day and night by the sentries of Cromwell's New Model Army.

CHAPTER 7

The Iron Grip of the Commonwealth

———➤●◄———

With the king now safely in his hands, Cromwell marched to London. There, he threw the Presbyterian members of the English parliament out of office and replaced them with Independents. Then, once in control of the government, he ordered the imprisonment of King Charles. He was held at Woburn, where, in a secret interview with the Scottish commissioners, he did at last consent to sign the Covenant and to unite with his Scottish subjects to expel the Independents, or Sectaries as they were now commonly called. Also, he made several appointments, including a provisional arrangement made on 20 July 1647 for Lord Balcarres to become Governor of Edinburgh Castle.

The news that at last, after nine years, the king, in the knowledge that his life was threatened, had agreed to sign the Covenant, was received with amazement, amounting to disbelief, by some members of the Scottish Parliament. Argyll, convinced that the king's conversion, known to have been made under pressure, was not sincere, formed a party of opposition known as the Remonstrators, or Protestors, against Charles's proposal that he would recognise Presbyterianism on probation for at least three years.

Against them, the great majority of the nation, headed by the Treasurer, Crawford-Lindsay, the Duke of Hamilton and Lord Balcarres, adhering to constitutional Royalism, formed themselves into a group which became known as the Resolutioners. Quickly they formed an Engagement, or League, to rescue the king. Hamilton, with an army of 14,000, marched into the north-west of England. A brave man, he fought valiantly but, outmatched as a strategist by Cromwell, he was totally defeated at Preston on 20 August 1648. Imprisoned, he was shortly afterwards beheaded after a summary trial.

The disastrous defeat at Preston ended the resistance of the king's party in Scotland. Argyll was now the ruling power. Cromwell entered Edinburgh on 4 October 1648. He insisted that all supporters of the Engagement must be turned out of office. Crawford-Lindsay was thus deprived of his position as High Treasurer and President of the Committee of Estates and Balcarres, no longer Governor of Edinburgh Castle, retired to Fife.

The news of the king's execution, which took place on Tuesday, 30 January 1649, spread with the speed of a hurricane through Scotland. People of all classes and in all walks of life were horrified to the depths of their souls. The majority of the populace wished to install the dead man's son as Charles II, but the Protestors, with Argyll at their head, would only agree to accept him on condition that he signed the Covenant. Charles, in exile at Breda in Holland, prevaricated. He had hopes that Montrose, who had left Holland for Scotland, would again achieve the success of his former brilliant campaign. This did not happen. Montrose, defeated in Sutherland, was taken prisoner at Loch Assynt and tried and executed in Edinburgh on 21 May. Charles, having sailed from Holland, did finally sign the Covenant, when still on board ship at the mouth of the Spey, on 23 June.

Only two months later, Cromwell marched north, intent on extending the republican government already established in England into Scotland. David Leslie, still in command of the Scottish army, believed that he had trapped Cromwell on the coast road between the Pentlands and the North Sea. But Leslie then made the mistake of leaving the high ground to attack and, on 3 September, he was outmanoeuvred and heavily defeated near Dunbar. King Charles, detesting the Covenanters, who railed at him much as they had at his father, is said to have secretly rejoiced at their enemy's success.

Following Leslie's defeat Argyll formed a coalition with the Resolutioners, or Constitutionalists, who included Crawford-Lindsay and Balcarres. Cromwell's forces now occupied most of Scotland south of the Forth and Clyde, but Argyll managed to reach an agreement with him and so retained control over most of the Highlands and the Isles. Argyll headed the committee that arranged the young king's coronation, which took place on 1 January 1651 in the old cathedral at Scone, hereditary place of the inauguration of Scottish kings. Charles wore magnificent robes and his pages were the sons of those nobles who adhered to the Covenant. He sat beneath a canopy of red velvet where, in accordance with ancient privilege, the crown was placed on his head by Argyll while Crawford-Lindsay put the sceptre in his hands. Only the traditional anointing was omitted, this being considered a superstitious rite.

Again in keeping with custom, the newly crowned Charles II bestowed honours upon his subjects. Alexander Balcarres, created an earl, was made Secretary of State and High Commissioner of the General Assembly of the Kirk. Some months later at St Andrews, where the Assembly convened in July, he proved himself so competent that the Assembly 'passed more acts in favour, and rose better satisfied with the king and Crown than any that had preceded in many years before'.[1]

However, not all were satisfied. The Protestors united in fury, howling out that the proceedings had been as 'the ripping up of the bowels of their mother Church'.[2] Balcarres was unrepentant, secure in the knowledge that he had achieved at least some unity between the Assembly and the king.

Following his coronation, the king made a royal progress through the parts of eastern and northern Scotland which were not under the control of Cromwell's Commonwealth army. At Pittenweem, on the Fife coast, church bells rang out in welcome as he came ashore. The baillies gave him a banquet and cannon roared a salute as he left the little town. From there the king moved on to Balcarres Castle where, on 22 February, as a Fifeshire chronicler reports, 'Lord Balcarres gave his majesty a banquet at his house, where he stayed some two hours, and visited his lady that then lay in'.[3]

This is the first mention of Countess Anna during those tumultuous years when she had lived quietly at Balcarres while her husband was so much occupied in serving his country and the Covenant for the king whose son they now honoured in their home. During this time her two younger daughters had been born, firstly Henrietta, whose date of birth is unknown, and then Sophia, who was christened at Kilconquhar on 6 October 1649. The joy of this occasion was lessened by the tragedy of losing another son. In much the same way as Anne's birth had followed the death of the first-born baby, David, in 1641, Sophia's arrival came a year after the death of another boy, named John.

But in 1651, heavily pregnant with another child, Countess Anna entertained the new king in the castle's dining hall; she is known to have made her entrance from the turnpike staircase coming directly from her bedroom.

Today the room, although now panelled with dark wood, remains so little changed that it is easy to picture the banquet taking place there over 350 years ago. It being still February, the shutters are drawn but the room is lit by the soft glow of wax candles and burning logs on the fire. Delicious smells rise from platters piled with roasts of beef and birds, borne in by servants who are scurrying back and forth. The finest wine from the cellar glints blood-red as it is poured. Silver plate (the last not yet sold for armaments) gleams down the length of the table set with places for many guests.

Amongst them the king, a dark-haired athletic young man, taller than most in the room, rises, as do the others, as Anna enters, big with child yet elegant in a voluminous gown. As shown in her portrait, she wears pearls around her throat with what appears to be a diadem of jewels above the ringlets of her glorious hair. Seating herself at the head of the table, with the king as guest of honour on her right, she notices his animation, the distinctive saturnine features, so often stern with anger, tonight alive with pleasure at the welcome he was receiving in Fife. He tells her of his growing confidence that with the people of Scotland behind him he will regain his father's throne in England. His excitement is infectious, so palpable that it spreads throughout the room. He rises, goblet in hand, drawing the rest of the diners to their feet, to drink toasts both to the success of his coming campaign and to his hostess, whose beauty he so plainly admires.

Almost a week later, when Anna's third son was born, the king agreed to be godfather to the little boy whom, in his honour, his parents named Charles.

*

King Charles, with his star rising in Scotland, was now convinced that in England the Royalists would join his cause. The Duke of Hamilton (the former Earl of Lanark, who had succeeded his brother following the latter's execution) agreed that an invasion of England was now the best course of action. Accordingly, the Scottish army left Stirling on 31 July and crossed the Tweed into England on 5 August 1651.

The king left the newly created Earl of Balcarres, together with the earls of Crawford-Lindsay, Marischal and Glencairn, as a Committee of Estates in charge of his affairs in Scotland.

Argyll, who had reached an agreement with Cromwell, did not join the Royal army, claiming that his wife was ill.

In the event he was proved, with his usual circumspection, to have made a sensible decision. King Charles, after a gallant struggle in which he himself fought with extreme heroism (he was lucky to survive), was totally defeated at Worcester on 3 September. After many adventures he managed to reach France but in Scotland, those who supported him were left to pay the price of their loyalty.

Foremost amongst those who suffered were Lord Crawford-Lindsay and the Earl Marischal who, almost immediately, were taken prisoner by General George Monck, Cromwell's commanding officer in Scotland. Crawford-Lindsay, held first in the Tower of London and later at Windsor Castle, remained a political prisoner in England for no fewer than nine years.

Alexander Balcarres, warned of what was happening, escaped to the Highlands. He probably headed west before turning north to bypass Cromwell's army at Perth. Once beyond the Tay, thanks to a long-standing friendship with the Earl of Huntly, he was virtually safe from pursuit. Then with Anna's uncle, Lord Seaforth, raising the MacKenzies in his support, he assumed the command of the Royalists under the king's commission.

*

Countess Anna, left once again at Balcarres, had to struggle with running the household in the most economical way she could achieve. Gone were the luxuries of satin and velvet gowns. Thanks to a now acute shortage of money, she and her children, like their servants, wore homespun cloth and shoes fashioned from hide by the local cobblers who plied their trade in country places.

The prime reason for their poverty was that Balcarres had

spent the then-enormous sum of £20,000 in raising and equipping his regiment of horse in 1643, but had never seen a penny of the promised recompense from the Committee of Estates. In addition to this, in the following year, he had provided a further sum of £500 sterling in the public service, the repayment of which the Committee had again ignored. Then, to make matters even worse, soldiers from other regiments of the Scottish army had been quartered on his land, which inevitably caused much destruction and theft.

Shortly after the king's visit Alexander had sold the remaining Balcarres plate. Known to have been unusually valuable, it raised £2,000. However, far from starting to pay off his debts, the sum had instead been used to cover the cost of the General Assembly in St Andrews, when visitors to his own neighbourhood had to be entertained. Lodgings, together with food for the delegates and their armed retinues, as well as stabling and fodder for their horses, had to be provided and, while the servants could make do with ale, the great lords and even their squires quaffed quantities of expensive imported wine.

Now, plagued as he already was with debt, Balcarres mortgaged his estates to provide the arms and ammunition as well as the payment of the soldiers of the king's army in the north.

Thus the estates of Balcarres which, when he had inherited them from his father in 1641, had been free of all encumbrance, were, by 1652, to a very large extent in the hands of guarantors. Balcarres had to provide dowries for his sisters (although his own wife's marriage settlement of over £20,000 Scots, owed to her since 1637, had never been paid by her uncle either as capital sum or even as interest accumulated over fifteen years).[4]

The extreme financial difficulty which the family faced is proved by a codicil to a will made by Alexander some short time later. In this he states that 'Lady Anna, my dearest spouse, hath out of her affection to me and for satisfying my urgent debts, quit and sold her jewels and womanly furniture, belonging to herself allanerly [only] by the law of this kingdom'. He therefore bequeaths her his precious collection of books, earmarked originally for his male heirs, worth 6,000 merks, together with all his household furniture, subject to redemption by his heirs at the above value, but otherwise to be her own in replacement of what she had so generously parted with for his relief.[5]

Most of Countess Anna's jewels had been left to her by her mother who, when she was dying, had given them to the charge of her husband to be divided between Anna and Jean, her two then very little girls, when they were grown up. Others must have been wedding gifts or else the objects of her so-called extravagance, so greatly disapproved of by her guardian Lord Rothes.

The Balcarreses, like so many other Scottish families, were brought to the verge of bankruptcy by the Civil War. Countess Anna was to struggle for years to obtain the promised reimbursement for all that she and her husband had lost for both the Covenant and the king. Her husband was to die almost penniless but she, thanks to the fortuitous marriage of her younger son to an heiress, was to see the estate in Fife redeemed.

On news of the king's defeat at Worcester, and that Charles had himself escaped, supposedly to France, Balcarres, coming to the sensible decision that further resistance was useless, surrendered to the English at Forres under honourable conditions on 3 December 1651.[6] Riding home to his impoverished family he was now most bitterly aware that all he had given of his inheritance in the service of his king and country had been sacrificed in vain.

CHAPTER 8

The Glencairn Rising

Alexander Balcarres returned to his home, but for some reason, probably financial, he and his family then lived in St Andrews, in the house of a Mr John Leper, a former provost of the town. Lord Lindsay says that the house stood 'under the shadow of the old cathedral towers, or what then remained of them, once the architectural glory of Scotland'.[1] From there they could see the damage done to the castle by a French fleet, summoned by Mary of Guise to avenge the murder of Cardinal Beaton by a party of Fife lairds, supporters of John Knox, in 1547. Now, over a hundred years later, the east wing of the castle was crumbling into the sea.

It was here that their fourth son, Colin, was born. Thankfully, he proved to be a healthy boy. He was baptised by the Reverend David Forret at Kilconquhar on 23 August 1642. Despite their financial worries Alexander and Anna Balcarres were grateful that at least the country was no longer at war. In St Andrews they lived peacefully with the children. Nonetheless Countess Anna was beset by a new worry for her husband who, plagued by fevers and a persistent cough, was plainly ill. Her anxiety increased when, as General Monck was recalled to England in 1653, the Royalists in the Highlands seized the chance to rise in arms.

The first word of trouble came from the Isle of Lewis, where Anna's uncle, Lord Seaforth, was joined by an English agent of King Charles, 'a black proper man' (a dark handsome man) called Crawford, as the Commonwealth commander-in-chief,

Colonel Robert Lilburne, described him.[2] Early in June *The Fortune*, a Commonwealth man-of-war commanded by a Captain Edwards, appeared off the island. A lieutenant and seven sailors, who went on shore to get fresh meat, were promptly kidnapped by the islanders. They were shortly released but Lilburne seized the opportunity to make an example of the MacKenzies by ordering the arrest of their chiefs. 'Undoubtedly to make the Lord Seaforth and his island (called the Lewes) exemplary will bee a very great advantage to the nation' said he with some malice.[3] Accordingly, a Colonel Cobbett sailed to the island with several frigates. They landed unmolested but then found that Lord Seaforth, having made some attempt to fortify Stornoway, with many of his chief men, had disappeared to mainland Scotland. His natural brother, left to govern the island, surrendered on Cobbett issuing an amnesty, but several companies of English soldiers were forthwith installed to guard the port of Stornoway against a possible attack by the navy of the Dutch, who were then at war with Cromwell.

Lilburne was soon proved to have been badly mistaken in thinking that by making scapegoats of the MacKenzies he had subdued opposition to Cromwell's domination of Scotland. The Earl of Atholl declared for King Charles, as also, to their father's grief and fury, did Archibald, Lord Lorne, and Lord Neil Campbell, sons of the Marquess of Argyll. Lord Lorne wrote from Inveraray on Thursday, 14 April to Lord Wilmot and to Charles II to assure them of his 'constant loyalty to his Majesty's royal persone, family, and government', and of his desire to do His Majesty service according to his power.[4]

Later that summer, Lorne joined a force led by Lord Kenmure, a notorious drinker who was always preceded by a man carrying a barrel of brandy known as Kenmure's drum. Marching down to Kintyre, they attacked the farmers from Ayrshire whom Lorne's father the Marquess had recently settled there. However, having taken some of their cattle, they did little damage to the property, which Lorne knew would one day be his own.

Returning from this expedition, he was confronted by his father, who demanded to know whether 'he was involved with these people now astir'.[5] Lorne assured him that he was not but then rode straight off to Glenorchy, where, in Kilchurn Castle, the home of his foster parents, Sir Robert Campbell and his wife, he met up with MacNaughton of Dunderave, Argyll's former chamberlain, Campbell of Auchinbreck, and Sir Arthur Forbes (later the Earl of Granard) 'and such are of that crew'.[6] Argyll was naturally utterly furious at the duplicity, and what he considered the treachery, of his son and heir. 'Let all the curse and judgments pronounced in God's word against disobedient children to parents come upon you . . . for you are a crosse (I may say a curse) to your father and a heavinesse to your mother, if you continue in your waies' he wrote, but Lorne was not to be moved.[7]

General John Middleton, having escaped from prison in his wife's clothes after being captured at the Battle of Worcester, had joined King Charles in France. The king had then commissioned him to command his army in Scotland but had also sent written word to the Earl of Glencairn, authorising him to act as deputy until Middleton, who was ill, could arrive.

Later, in October, Charles was to write to Alexander Balcarres, explaining why he had sent the commission to Glencairn and not to himself. 'As well as your own letters has the relation of Sir William Bellenden gave me great apprehension of your want of health, nor have there wanted reports of your death, so that I had no hopes that you would have been able to have ventured into the Highlands.'[8]

But the king had mistaken his man. Balcarres, whose now obvious illness would have made the perfect excuse to stay at home, bluntly and angrily, in view of what then appeared to him to be the king's insult, insisted on obeying his call to arms.

Countess Anna, who must have pleaded with him to forego such an obviously dangerous and, under the circumstances, foolish decision, finding him totally obstinate, then insisted on going with him on campaign.

In doing so she flaunted convention. It was rare, in fact almost unheard of, for a woman of her rank to share in the danger, not to mention the physical privation, inevitable on campaign even in civilised country far less the Highland wilds. Alexander may have tried to dissuade her. Perhaps David Forret lent his voice. But if so it was a wasted effort. Anna, always strong-willed, was adamant. Her courage and fear for her husband overruled all commonsense.

Once again the old castle of Balcarres echoed to the sound of tramping feet and shouting voices as the fencible men came in to be equipped with weapons and targes from the armoury. Then, when assembled, the regiment set forth. It was led by the cavalry, the men in protective breastplates, swords strapped to their sides. Behind them marched the foot soldiers, armed mainly with pikes and axes. They were followed by strings of pack-horses bearing the tents and provisions, including sacks of oatmeal, walking head to tail. Last of all came the cooks and the camp followers, who, from time immemorial, follow an army on the move.

Heading north from Fife they most probably bypassed the English-occupied city of Perth to be ferried across the Tay at Inver, the main crossing place over the river before the building of Telford's bridge further downstream. From there they would have pushed on, past the confluence of the Tay and the Garry at Ballinluig. Then, after following the east bank of the latter river though the Pass of Killiecrankie, they would have crossed over the west end of the Grampians to come down into the valley of the Spey.

*

The Royalist army gathered in Lochaber where, so Lilburne was informed, about 1200 men were assembled between Lochaber and Inverness. Countess Anna lived like the soldiers, sometimes, wrapped in a plaid, even sleeping on bare ground or at best on a pile of heather or straw. In the worst of the weather, however, she and her husband, particularly in view of his poor health, must have sheltered in a tent or in one of the makeshift huts roofed with turf or heather, as was common in army camps. For washing there was only water drawn in leather buckets from the burns where, on fine days, her clothes were scrubbed on flat rocks before being hung up to dry. As the cold intensified, coating the pools with ice, some water for her to wash in may have been heated over a fire.

While porridge, boiled in iron cauldrons, was the basic food of everyone in the camp, both cattle and sheep were slaughtered to be roasted on spits over the fires. Nothing was ever wasted. Men reared to hard living made broth out of every bone. Liver and kidneys, and even blood mixed with oatmeal, were life-savers against both hunger and cold.

Even more essentially, while the officers warmed themselves and no doubt found brief respite from discomfort with wine and brandy, the men scoured the country for home-brewed ale and the highly potent *uisge beatha*, the Gaelic name for the original whisky, distilled secretly in Highland glens.

Most of the time Anna probably rode a horse or a pony with a ghillie at its head, but in places too rough or precipitous for horses, she hitched up her skirts like those of the country-women as she waded through boggy ground and over burns. She must have been physically strong and, although she had had six children, she was still only thirty-two. Certainly no mention is made of her being ill on what must have been a dangerous adventure but, raised as she had been in Ross-shire, the sound of men talking in Gaelic and the smell of peat burning on camp fires must have brought back familiar memories of her childhood at Brahan.

The campaign began with great enthusiasm. The Balcarreses were cheered by the companionship of Sir Robert Moray,
who had married Alexander's sister, Lady Sophia, and was also
his closest friend. Furthermore, they became well acquainted
with Lord Lorne and his brother, Lord Neil Campbell.

Archibald, Lord Lorne, was then a young man of twenty-
five. Small in stature, he had the violent temper of a bantam
cock. Relations between the Campbells and MacDonalds,
hereditary enemies as they were, had been worsened by
Alasdair MacColla MacDonald's destruction of Argyll's country during the recent Civil War. Unfortunately, on arriving at
the camp, almost the first person he saw was MacDonnell of
Glengarry, a man as irascible as himself. The two flew at each
other like wild-cats, both drawing their swords. Fortunately
friends on both sides were quick enough to haul them apart.
Nonetheless, as Lilburne reported to Cromwell, with some
satisfaction, 'they were prevented from fighting, yet parted
great enemies'.[9]

This would seem to have been Lorne's first introduction to
Countess Anna, and subsequent events were to prove that he
had then become enchanted by the beautiful wife of Lord
Balcarres. He was not her only admirer. Her courage and spirit
as she endured the torrential rain of the Highlands, the poor
food and almost total absence of comfort, with only the care of
her husband in her mind, incited respect and admiration in
many another man's heart.

Sadly, as Balcarres – with his knowledge of the pride and
jealousy of Highland chiefs – had foreseen, these autocrats
soon began to quarrel amongst themselves. It did not help that
the man chosen by the king to lead them pending Middleton's
arrival came from the Lowlands, to the Highlanders an inferior
and different world. William, 9th Earl Glencairn, head of the
ancient Ayrshire family of Cunningham, was then a man of
forty-three. He did have military experience. Sent by Charles I

to Ireland in 1641 to defend the Ulster colonists, he had afterwards been made Privy Councillor of the Treasury. Although lacking the authority of a great leader, he still saw himself as another Montrose. He wanted to emulate the achievements of the man who had so nearly won Scotland for King Charles I by invading the Lowlands, where, particularly in Ayrshire, he knew he would find support.

Balcarres, however, knowing that Glencairn's small, untrained army could not possibly contend with General Monck's regimented and experienced troops, argued forcibly that they should remain in the comparative safety of the Highlands 'until they should see what assistance the king could procure them from beyond sea of men, money and arms; whereas if they went out of their fast grounds, they could not hope to stand before such a veteran and well-disciplined army as Monck had and, if they met with the least check, their tumultuary army would soon melt away'.[10]

The army, in fact, was disappearing fast. In December the quick-tempered Lord Lorne had another furious quarrel, this time with Glencairn. Incandescent with fury, Lorne, with his Campbell contingent, then left the Royalist camp.[11]

News of the controversy between the leaders of his army and of Glencairn's apparent indecision as to his plans of attack reached the king in France. Charles then wrote to Balcarres, the one man whom he felt that he could really trust, saying that he was 'perplexed with contradictory reports'. Apparently unaware of Balcarres' continuing illness and of the extent and difficulty of the journey he was asking him to undertake, he asked him 'to repair to him for that purpose with all possible speed'.[12]

It was now the depth of winter. Snow had fallen heavily and the temperature frequently plunged as low as nine or ten degrees below zero. The tracks over the mountains were almost impassable. Lord Lindsay describes the journey:

[through] a tract of the enemies' country of above four or five hundred miles, he consulted as little the difficulties and dangers as he had done before, but rendered immediate obedience, and put himself and his dear lady (whose virtue and kindness would never abandon him in his greatest extremity) both in disguise, and, with the often perils of their lives, at last by God's providence arrived safely in France, where, having with great integrity on his own and as great satisfaction on the King's part given his Majesty a perfect account and enforced on him the necessity of sending over some military man to whom the confederated chiefs would submit more willingly than to one of their own order, Middleton was dispatched to Scotland.[13]

It would seem that Alexander and Anna, having left Lochaber, somehow made their way firstly to Fife. They must have needed clothes other than the thick rough garments, now probably stained with mud and peat, which they had worn on the campaign. Also, more importantly, they had to make arrangements for the children who had been left behind during the campaign.

The three girls – Anne, born in 1642, and now twelve, Henrietta, a few years younger and Sophia, who was only four – despite the danger of the journey, apparently went with them to France. Anne is certainly mentioned later and the sympathy offered to Lady Balcarres and her 'little ones' certainly suggests that they were with her at the time of her husband's death.[14]

Heartbreakingly, however, the two little boys, Charles, aged two and Colin, just a year old, the precious heirs, were thought too young for such a long and perilous journey and had to be left behind in the care of the good Mr Forret. It was a sensible decision, particularly in the circumstances. Anna and Alexander, although very deeply distressed at the parting as they are known to have been, believed they would soon be back. They could not have foreseen, or even guessed at, the length of their absence abroad. Neither could they have surmised, as they held the little boys in their arms before handing them over to the minister, who promised to care for them as his own, that Alexander would never see them again.

CHAPTER 9

The Royal Court in Exile

———➤●◄———

It was some consolation to Alexander and Anna Balcarres that their brother-in-law, Sir Robert Moray – a man universally popular – went with them on their long journey to Paris. His affection is shown by his nicknames for them both. Alexander's was Gossip, 'a godfather', while Anna he called 'Cummer', an old Scottish word for woman. Lord Lindsay says that they travelled 'in disguise, and with often the peril of their lives'.[1] He does not specify, because he probably did not know, at least in detail, how they managed to conceal their identity. However, it seems safe to guess that they probably rode on rough Highland ponies, such as were used to pull ploughs, and muffled themselves in thick cloaks, necessary in any case to protect them against gale-driven rain and snow. Anna's cloak must have been hooded, to hide her glorious hair, while Alexander may have worn a bonnet, like most of the local men. Also, in all probability, he hid much of his face below a beard.

With them went their three daughters, some essential luggage and almost certainly a few trusted servants, all muffled in heavy plaids such as the country people wore and travelling in some sort of inconspicuous conveyance, most likely a farm cart. Anne, at fourteen years old, may have been old enough to ride but her younger sisters, Henrietta and Sophia, must have made the journey in some form of horse-drawn vehicle.

Heading south they faced many dangers, but ironically it

was now safer to travel in Britain than it had been for centuries before. Thanks to the Commonwealth government, the highwaymen and cutthroats who had formerly threatened the roads had been, for the most part, hanged, exported or placed behind bars. Lord Lindsay also writes that 'they travelled through a tract of the enemies' country of above four or five hundred miles', which indicates that they may have sailed from Hull, or one of the other shipping ports of England's north-east coast.

The voyage itself must have been hazardous even if, unlikely in early spring, the weather was kind. Notoriously, the high-sided wooden sailing ships, if not actually wrecked, were frequently driven miles off-course, often to a destination other than that intended, while battling across the North Sea.

Reaching Paris in May 1654 Alexander at once went to the Palais Royal, where he gave a letter to the exiled King Charles. The document, headed by the signature of Countess Anna's uncle, the Earl of Seaforth, also bore those of Lord Lorne, the famous Evan Dhu, or Black Sir Evan Cameron of Lochiel, Roderick MacLeod, nicknamed 'the Witty', chief of the MacLeods of Skye, Sir Roderick of Scallascarr, or Talisker, MacLeod's uncle, and the leader of the clan during his minority, MacLeod of Raasay, 'Daniel' (or Donald) MacLean, the uncle of Sir Hector of Duart, the young chief who had been killed fighting gallantly at Inverkeithing, the MacLeans of Coll and Ardgour, and the chiefs of MacKinnon and MacNachtan. 'Testifying to his own and Sir Robert's merits, and requesting the King to give implicit credit to whatever they might report and represent in relation to the royal cause and public service.'[2]

Balcarres, whose counsels, as Lord Lindsay says, 'always varied [with] the occasion – prudent and cautious when supporting Baillie and controlling Glencairn, bold and daring when an emergency like the present demanded it'[3] – strongly urged on the king the expediency of sailing for the Highlands and taking command of the clans in person, on the principle afterwards adopted by Prince Charles Edward, the 'Young Chevalier', in 1745. He spoke with authority and the king listened to him, knowing that he was supported by the earls of Lauderdale and Crawford-Lindsay, now both political prisoners in England, but still able to communicate with him by letters written in code which were smuggled out, usually by means of bribery, to the jailers or the washer-women of the castles in which they were held.

Charles hesitated, however, afraid to commit himself to a venture which, if it went wrong, would probably cost him his life. Nine years earlier, in 1646, the now outlawed Ludovic, the 'Loyal' Earl of Crawford, in conjunction with the Irish, had suggested much the same plan to rescue Charles I. The queen, Henrietta Maria, and her chief advisor Lord Jermyn, however, had then refused to countenance the plan, believing it to be too dangerous in the absence of guaranteed support. Now, for the same reasons and, as Lord Lindsay says, 'his irresolution and love of ease',[4] their son prevaricated, the result being fatal delay. Had Charles gone at once to Scotland as Balcarres urged him to do, he might have galvanised his supporters to drive the Commonwealth army of occupation from Scotland. But Argyll, the cleverest and most potent leader of the west and central parts of the country, was against them and Charles, through his indecision, probably avoided a debacle. The idea of the king's return to Scotland was finally abandoned when news reached Paris of Middleton's total and disastrous defeat at Dalnaspidal, near the head of Loch Garry, on 19 July 1654.

News of the rout filtered over to Holland. Countess Anna's uncle, the Earl of Seaforth, surrendered on 10 January 1655. In April General Monck asked the Marquess of Argyll to tell his son Lord Lorne that, 'if he brought in MacNaughton it would improve his own fate' and they both surrendered on 17 May.[5] Other Highland chiefs followed suit, some of them consequently being allowed to raise guards, known as watches, to protect their own people against the looting and lifting of cattle which, in the confused state of the country, were a menace day and night.

Meanwhile, on 4 January of the previous year, the Balcarres estates in Scotland had been sequestered by an Act of Parliament so that the Earl and Countess, with their three young daughters, were now near-penniless refugees.

It must have been of some small comfort if word reached them from Scotland that the sum of £10 a year had been allowed from the forfeited estate for the upkeep of their two little sons. Only later was Anna to find how, for the first four years they were abroad, even this small sum had been withheld. Mr Forret, although eventually compensated, had somehow provided for them himself out of his small salary which, thanks to the banishment of the main proprietors of the parish, can hardly have been more than a pittance.

*

Desperate as was the plight of the Balcarreses, King Charles himself was in much the same state. Denied much of the pension promised him by the French government, he was exploited by Cardinal Mazarin as a political pawn. When Lord and Lady Balcarres reached Paris the king was still living with his mother, Queen Henrietta Maria, in the Louvre. We do not know whether the Balcarres family were housed in the same building or whether they were lodged elsewhere, but perhaps it was at this time that their eldest daughter Anne, an impressionable young girl brought up by her parents in the strict Presbyterian faith, first came under the spell of the fascinating and devout Roman Catholic queen.

This is the first indication that Anne was already obsessed with religious fervour. Plainly she was vulnerable, unsure of herself and seeking guidance, thus a ready victim for a power-fully manipulative woman. She seems to have been mesmerised by the glamour and sophistication of the French-born queen. Probably she saw her as an icon while the queen, for her part, used all her influence to win her to what she herself believed to be the only true Christian faith. One can but pity poor Anne in her predicament. Approaching puberty, she may have felt antagonistic towards her mother, who, occupied as she was with a sick husband and Anne's two younger sisters, had little time for the problems of an emotional and highly strung young girl. The dilemma for Anne was intensified by her father's intolerance of the Catholic faith. Balcarres was 'taken for the head of the Presbyterians, or Scottish Constitutionalists. He held the office of Secretary of State for Scotland, and was employed in various political negotiations at Paris and else-where in the king's service'.[6]

Whatever their situation there, the Balcarreses' stay in the French capital was short. By the summer of 1654, the war between the English Commonwealth and the Dutch had ended and Mazarin was negotiating with Oliver Cromwell, now the Lord Protector of England, who was believed to have his eyes on the Crown. An alliance between England and France was a possibility. The Cardinal suddenly found the exiled king an embarrassment. Therefore he promised him the full payment of his French pension provided he left the country within the space of ten days.

Charles' departure, at such short notice, was little short of chaotic. His possessions, household goods and all, were loaded into carts pulled by his carriage horses while he himself rode out of Paris on horseback heading for the town of Spa, then in the Spanish Netherlands, some twenty-five miles south-east of the Belgian city of Liège. His little court, which included his former tutor and now censorious councillor Sir Edward Hyde, the Marquess of Ormonde, and the Balcarreses, followed him on roads which ran north-east through the valleys of the Oise, the Sambre and the Meuse.

The little party of refugees had small reason to celebrate, but it was now high summer and they danced through the afternoons. Then, after supper, probably to the music of local fiddlers scraping away at violins, they danced again in the meadows, far into the short nights. Another amusing distraction was bathing in Caesar's Bath.[7] At Spa the king's spirits were raised when he was joined by his eldest sister Mary, who as a child bride of nine had been sent to Holland to marry Prince William, Stadtholder of Orange. Mary, still in her early twenties, was a widow, her husband having died in 1650, six days before she gave birth to a son, who she named for his father.

The king's joy at seeing his sister so greatly lifted his depression that those in his attendance felt their own troubles to some extent lift away. The two chief hotels in Spa were occupied by the courts of the brother and sister and from this it would seem that Lord and Lady Balcarres were amongst those people who managed partly to forget their sorrows, if only for a few summer days.

*

Alexander and Anna Balcarres were now acutely embarrassed for money. Their situation became increasingly desperate, until Princess Mary, it would seem at the instigation of her mother, Queen Henrietta Maria, came to their aid. She could not lend them money, but she guaranteed a loan from Holland which made it possible for them to exist.

From Spa the king and his sister moved to Aachen, where they stayed for about a month before going on to Cologne. There, in what was then an independent archbishopric, they were welcomed by the city magistrates and much entertained.

The ancient German city, founded on the Rhine by the Romans, was dominated by the Gothic cathedral of St Peter and St Mary, dating from 1248, which housed, amongst other treasures, the golden shrine of the three magi as well as St Peter's staff and chain.

Despite the distractions of the city, it was here that Alexander Balcarres had his first clash with Sir Edward Hyde, who seems to have grown jealous over his increasing friendship with the king. 'No one', wrote Balcarres' grandson, 'had more favour, being cheerful as well as good and wise.'[8] Balcarres' good nature and optimism were all the more remarkable given that at this time, as the pall of a hard winter closed over Germany, he was extremely ill. The remarkable spirit of one so resilient to misfortune shines like a light down the centuries to prove him to have been an exceptional man. His very integrity, however, was enough to infuriate Hyde, intensely ambitious and ever suspicious of anyone who might in any way undermine his dominance over King Charles. Hyde was also head of the High Church party and Alexander's Presbyterianism in itself was enough to prompt his distrust. Somehow – Lord Lindsay does not tell us the details, of which he was probably ignorant himself – Hyde managed to contrive a confrontation between Balcarres and the king, as the result of which Balcarres was dismissed from the court.[9]

This was a very bad moment for both Alexander Balcarres and his wife, who, refugees as they were with little financial support, now lost the status of attachment to the king's entourage. Charles himself, however, was soon to realise his mistake. The courtiers were quarrelling and most were highly disgruntled because their salaries, such as they were, had not for some time been paid. The king, writing to Lord Arlington, said, 'Our little court are all at variance, but Lord Balcarres will soon return and heal us with his wisdom.'[10]

Lord Balcarres did come back, but before long he was again

at loggerheads with Hyde. This time it was because Countess Anna had been given the post of *gouvernante*, or nursery governess, to the little Prince William of Orange, Princess Mary's son. This position carried a small salary which, in their present straitened circumstances, was a godsend to the Balcarres family. The appointment seems to have been made at the instigation of Queen Henrietta Maria who, as the daughter of Henry IV of France and widow of Charles I of England, retained some standing in France and was in close contact with her daughter. Although largely impoverished herself – she had sold even her jewels to buy guns for her late husband's cause – she was nonetheless extremely kind to the Balcarres family, as Lord Lindsay reports.

Mary's son, now aged eight, was, through her, in line for the English throne. Countess Anna, whose own youngest daughter, Lady Sophia, was only nine, was delighted to look after the little boy, who was much the same age as her own two small sons, living in far-off Scotland and from whom she had now been parted for what must have seemed to be an interminable four years. Hyde, however, was furious, seeing this as an attempt to imbue the boy with the ethics of the Presbyterian religion. He raged so long and so furiously that for a time he implanted doubts in the king's mind as to whether the appointment of Lady Balcarres as governess was misplaced.

News of these ructions within the court filtered over to Scotland for, in a letter of 11 November 1658, the Glasgow Divine, Robert Baillie,* declaimed 'What is become of the king and his family we do not know, some talks that he should be in the Hague; many take his unkindness to Balcarres very ill,

---

* Robert Baillie, Scholar and Divine. Professor of Divinity at Glasgow, he had been one of the delegates sent to Holland in 1649 to persuade Charles II to return to Scotland to accept the Covenant and the Crown. Following the Restoration in 1661 he became Principal of Glasgow University, hence as 'Principal' he then became commonly known.

especially that he should oppose his lady's provision to the oversight [governance] of the little Prince of Orange; his obstinate observance of Hyde offends us all.' Subsequently, in 1659, he writes 'I am not yet satisfied with Hyde's very unjust breaking of his neck – God will see to it.'[11]

The movements of the Balcarres family from place to place then become obscure until, from 1657 to 1658, they are known to have been in Holland, living at the Hague. Here the court was dominated by the presence of two beautiful women, the Princess Mary of Orange and her even more illustrious aunt, Elizabeth of Bohemia, known to posterity as the 'Winter Queen'.

Elizabeth, who was the eldest daughter of King James VI & I, was now sixty-one. An old lady by the standards of those days, she nonetheless retained much of the dignity of presence and the captivating charm which all of her chroniclers describe. In a portrait painted by the artist Robert Peake just before her marriage to Frederick V, then Elector of the Palatinate, she wears a virginal white dress, the skirts spread over a farthingale, a high lace collar framing a young face, with the high brow typical of her Stuart ancestry. Round her neck hang three strings of pearls, and jewels are set into her high-piled glorious auburn hair.

Elizabeth had known much tragedy. Within six years of their marriage her husband, having been offered the crown of Bohemia, had been deposed after six months. Thus she became known as the 'Winter Queen'. They had fled to Holland where, with the sanction of the Stadtholder of Orange, they had been given sanctuary in the Hague. Frederick, her husband, had died in 1632. Her sons, who had fought so gallantly for their uncle, Charles I, had been exiled from Britain by Cromwell. Prince Maurice had been drowned at sea in 1654 and his more famous brother, Prince Rupert, inheritor both of his mother's looks and charismatic charm, was now a privateer in the West Indies hoping to make a fortune in what was then a lucrative trade.

Countess Anna, who knew what it was to lose children, two of her sons having died as infants, would come to have even more in common with Elizabeth of Bohemia when her eldest daughter, also Elizabeth, refused to marry, choosing instead to become a nun. Anna, at this point, seems to have been unaware that her own daughter, Anne, who may have been influenced by the young Elizabeth, was planning to do the same.

Meanwhile, in 1658, Countess Anna was relieved to find that the sea air of the Hague improved her husband's health. Also the companionship of so many compatriots helped to reduce the sense of loss and consequent depression which, despite his outward forbearance, must have weighed heavily on his mind. Foremost amongst the Balcarres' acquaintances at this time were Cornelius van Sommerdyck, Lord of that Ilk, whose daughter Veronica was soon to be married to Alexander Bruce, afterwards Earl of Kincardine and, as Lord Lindsay says, 'predecessor of the late Earl of Elgin and Kincardine, Governor-General of India'.[12] That the friendship between the two families became very close is indicated by a letter to Bruce from Sir Robert Moray, Alexander's greatest friend and brother-in-law, shortly after Alexander's death. 'Say to your father-in-law that he hath me in my dear Gossip's [Balcarres] place as far as I can fill it; and if I were not his upon [that] account, his kindness to my dear Cummer [Lady Balcarres] is enough to make me so; and he may be sure he has me, and yet the more that I was very much so before.'[13]

In the summer of 1659 Alexander Balcarres again became very ill. Indications are that he suffered from tuberculosis, brought on, it was supposed, by the strain of marching and sleeping out on the mountains in bad weather during the Glencairn Rising in 1653. Now once again he defied his physical frailty with that wonderful spirit and serenity which so much inspired those who came into contact with this deeply religious man. The author of an obituary memoir wrote, 'During the last twelvemonth of his life, he spent with such advantage to his own soul and the edification of others, that there are many yet living that will, with all gratitude, acknowledge their conversation with him, his heavenly discourse and holy example, put them much into the way of following him thither.'[4]

*

Despite his apparent tranquility, the failure of the king's cause in Scotland, together with the uncertain future of his wife and family, apparently weighed heavily on Balcarres' mind. Then, in addition to these worries, another disagreement with the king, doubtless engineered by Hyde, made it necessary for him and his wife and their children to leave the court at the Hague. Balcarres, despite this treatment, remained unwaveringly loyal to the point where news of the failure of a rising by the Royalist Sir George Booth, in August 1659, was believed, certainly in Scotland, to have actively hastened his death.

Certainly the end was rapid for, on Tuesday, 7 September, or according to the new style on 30 August,* at Breda, he died in his wife's arms.

Again we have evidence, in her own words, of Anna's physical strength. Writing from the Hague some seven weeks later, she tells how during Alexander's last month no one had been allowed to move him but herself. Her handwritten description is one of the earliest papers of Anna Lindsay, Countess of Balcarres, held in the Crawford collection now in the National Library of Scotland.

* The 'new style' refers to the Gregorian Calendar, that is, the regulation of the year according to the reformation introduced by Pope Gregory XIII in 1582. It was only adopted in Scotland in 1752.

The recipient of the letter, dated 31 October, was Colonel Sir James Henderson, one of the Hendersons of Fordell, who was a dear friend both of Alexander Balcarres and herself. It is proof of their utter devotion to each other from the time when they were first married nineteen years before. Then, when Anna had come as a bride to the prosperous estate of Balcarres, their future had seemed so secure. Few could have visualised what would happen, but adversity, so often the destruction of a marriage, had in fact cemented their own. Neither, at a time when adultery was so commonplace that lovers and mistresses were *de rigueur*, did either of them, as far as is known, even contemplate an extramarital liaison.

Alexander's death at the comparatively early age of forty-one, an exile from the country for which he had lost all he owned, is a tragedy on its own. It is made even more so by Anna's grief, heartbreaking in its intensity, which still clutches at one's throat as one reads the letter, penned in the stylistic handwriting of over 350 years ago.

My noble and dear Cousin,

I could not leave this place without saying somewhat to your lady and you of the sense I have of your civilities and kindness to me and that dear saint of mine that is now in glory. I know you are both sharers with me in this my sad loss I sustain in the want of one of the worthiest men in the world and the kindest husband. Therefore I shall tell you that you, and I, and all that belongs to him have reason to rejoice that we have had such a subject to mourn for, since his goodness, the means that heightened his glory, is the object of that impatience which afflicts us. I assure you, he died as he lived, full of courage, and piety, and patience, and tenderness to me, and affection to his friends, and charity to his enemies.

Because I know how well you loved him, I shall tell you a little of what he said before the Lord took him. Upon the

Wednesday in the morning he called me and prayed me that I would not be troubled with what he was to tell me, which was that he could rise up no more. He had sat up and gone upon his feet until that time only to keep me from sad apprehensions of approaching death to him – or rather I may say, life to him, joyful to him, though sad to me. When he saw me troubled, he said, 'My dear, why do you break my heart? You ought to rejoice because I say, as my blessed saviour did, I go to my Father – ay, said he, 'and your Father; and because I go from persecution and calumny to that company of angels and the spirits of just men made perfect.' Upon the Friday he said to me, 'My dear I have got good news to tell you; I have overcome my greatest difficulty' – 'My love,' said I, 'what's that?' Said he, 'To part with my dear! Now I can leave you, for I have given you up to the Father, who, I am confident, will care for you.' Oh me! What that dear mouth said of me, and what I was, and what I had been to him, I am not able to relate, though it was fit for me!

That day he made a long prayer for the King, that the Lord would bless him with principles fit for him; and a great deal more he said to this purpose; and also he prayed for the rest of the royal family, and for all his friends, particularly by name, that had been true and kind to him in his afflictions, and that God would forgive his enemies . . .

The last eight days of that dear life I may say his dear heart was always in heaven, for he was almost always praying, or hearing prayer, or reading, or speaking to the praise of his blessed maker and Redeemer. There was with him one Mr Forbes, a minister and a very honest man, who professed that in all his life he never was so happy nor got so much good out of anything as in being with my dear at this time.

I sat always upon the carpet before his bed-side, and often I looked in to him, and when I found not his eyes fixed upon heaven, I spake to him.

Upon the Lord's day I asked him what he was doing, and said, 'My love, have you attained to that great measure of assurance that you desire?' – To which he answered, 'I can not tell what they call for assurance, but this I can tell you, that I am as full of joy in believing that my Redeemer is mine and I am his as I can hold, and that I shall be with him before it be long, and that he will never leave me' – 'That's good news, my dear,' said I, 'for you.' – 'Aye,' said he, 'and for you also,' said he, 'for you will quickly follow me' – 'Aye, my dear,' said I, 'you will not think it long, for a thousand years where you are going is but as Yesterday when it is past.'

Not a quarter of an hour before the Lord took him, he said to me with a strong voice (for the Lord gave him the use of his senses, and that great judgement he blessed him with, to the very last moment), 'My dear, I follow a good guide, he will never leave me, and I will never quit him'

I finding death fast approaching, I told him his Lord was fast making ready, attended with his blessed angels, to attend him to the mansion he had prepared for him before the world was, and that he would go with him through the valley of the shadow of death. At this he drew in my head to him and took the last farewell, which you may easily imagine sad to me, and said, 'My dear, pray the passage may be easy.'

After that, he prayed a little, looking whither he was going, laid those dear eyes together, and so went to his Redeemer out of my poor arms without the least motion. I stayed by him, and dressed him all myself, which he expected from me – for a month before that he would not eat nor drink but that I gave, nor would not let anybody stir him but I. At last I closed those dear eyes, and that dear mouth I never in all my life heard make a lie or take the name of God in vain. Oh! How Christianly that dear saint of mine lived and died it is impossible for me to tell you as it was! This will satisfy you that I have said, so as to let you know your friend lives for ever.

To tell you of my disconsolate condition is but unnecessary to you who know how great reason I have. I hope this separation will help to order my steps to the like passage to that place where my dear saint has gone before me.

It is now near the time my letter must go, so I will no more but to present my most kind respects to your worthy good lady and to your sister, my Lady Stencalven;* and to desire you to believe, wherever I am I shall be, in the sense of all your favours,

Noble Cousin,
Your very affectionate Cousin
And humble servant,
Anne Balcarres
This next week I intend, God willing, to leave this place.[15]

Amongst the many obituaries which testify to the outstanding character of Alexander, Lord Balcarres, is that of Robert Baillie, who describes him as 'one of the most brave and able gentlemen of our nation, if not the most able'.[16] Likewise, the liberal thinker Richard Baxter called him 'a lord of excellent learning, judgment and honesty, none being praised equally with him for learning and understanding in all Scotland'.[17] Even more voluble was the poet Cowley, who, in a long elegy following Balcarres' death, wrote:

> His wisdom, justice, and his piety,
> His courage, both to suffer and to die,
> That once with so much industry and art
> Had clos'd the gaping wounds of every part,
> To perfect his distracted nation's cure.[18]

* This name seems to be written 'Stencolvis' by Lord Kellie in 1661. Writing to Lauderdale from Gouderoy in April, he says, 'My Lady Stencolvis, Colonel Henderson's sister, who is now at this place, presents her service to your Lordship and my Lady. Your Lordship was once in her house at Maestricht. She is really a very able lady, and my good friend.'

Alexander's embalmed body, sent home to Scotland, was landed at Elie on 2 December 1659. From there it was taken home to Balcarres. The funeral was delayed however, both because Countess Anna had not yet returned and also because, at this time, most people in Scotland were on tenterhooks, as rumour spread of the now expected return and Restoration of King Charles II.

CHAPTER 10

'I Am Not the Possessor of Sixpence'

———————•◀●◀———————

Meanwhile, back in the autumn of 1659, Sir Robert Moray, the Balcarres' old friend, was greatly concerned as to how Anna, with little or no money, would herself survive once her husband was dead. Writing to Alexander Bruce from Paris on 12 September 1659, he said:

Let us henceforward converse and speak as calmly of what concerns my dear Cummer as we can, and get her to do so too. My undoubting expectation [that] your next will tell me my dear Gossip hath shaken off mortality makes me think of what concerns my dear Cummer and her little ones; and here I give you not only mine own thoughts but my Lord Jermyn's, that no time may be lost in determining what is fit for her to do. I do not know in what portion of his estate she is infeft, nor whether her infestment is unbroken, nor where it is; but I think it will be necessary to prepare as soon as possible for a journey home to settle what concerns it and her little ones, and the estate. Her way must be by London, for which either she needs no pass, or may get Downings [Sir George Downing, as he later became, was then Resident of Ambassador from the Commonwealth to Holland]. There she will get Lauderdale's advice* and may procure what is

* Lauderdale, held in the Tower from 1651, was nonetheless, as a political prisoner, allowed both to correspond with and to receive visitors by arrangement.

necessary for taking off sequestration, &c, unless she determines otherwise. If there be any inconvenience in carrying the little ones [her daughters] with her, they may be left where they are, especially if she have any thought of coming back to be about the P.R. [the Princess Royal or Princess of Orange], which will be secured to her the while. I know not indeed how she will be provided for the journey unless you help her in it; yet I think the Queen [Henrietta Maria] will do somewhat in it, if she stay so long as it might be got done; for I would have her gone before winter.[1]

It would seem from her letter to Colonel Henderson, written on 31 October, in which she told him that 'This next week, God willing, I intend to leave this place', that Anna had already acquired enough money to travel to London. Most probably it came from a present, or else from another loan, arranged perhaps by the Princess Royal at the instigation of her mother Queen Henrietta Maria. On 19 September the queen, on hearing of Lord Balcarres' death, had written her a very kind letter. Having first expressed her great admiration for him, she had said that it would give her great pleasure 'to contribute anything to her consolation'.[2] Henrietta Maria had also written to her daughter, the Princess of Orange, in much the same vein. Countess Anna then wrote to the Princess from England, thanking her for her past kindnesses, as is revealed by a letter she had in return once she was back in Holland:

My Lady Balcarres,

If it had been in my power, you should have found before this time the effects of that true esteem I have for your person, for I may assure you with truth that the want of those occasions did much trouble me, and now more than ever, finding how much you are satisfied with those very little civilities I was able to perform when I was with you, which I am so ashamed you should take notice of that I will leave this subject, and tell you that the kindness of the Queen's invitation of me to come to her is very well able alone to overcome all endeavours of hindering me from that happiness, if I had not a most passionate desire of waiting upon her Majesty, which I hope to do very shortly in spite of all designs to the contrary; and wherever I go, let me desire you to believe that I shall always strive to show you the reality of my being, My Lady Balcarres,

Your most affectionate friend,
Marie.[3]

This letter was shortly followed by one from the king himself. Dated Brussels, 29 March 1660, he says:

Madame

I hope you are so well persuaded of my kindness to you as to believe that there can be no misfortune happen to you and I have not my share in it. I assure you I am troubled at the loss you have had; and I hope that God will be pleased to put me into such a condition before it be long as I may let you see the care I intend to have of you and your children, and that you may depend upon my being very truly, Madame,

Your affectionate friend,
Charles R.[4]

Countess Anna, by the time she received these letters from the king and his sister, had already returned from her brief visit to London. She stayed there in the November of 1659 only long enough to arrange family business before coming back to Holland and 'the little ones', her daughters. Lady Anne, the eldest, was seventeen, Lady Henrietta a few years younger and Lady Sophia, only ten.

It was anxiety over Anne, who had been presumably looking

after her sisters, rather than concern about the younger children, that brought Countess Anna back with such speed. Rumour had reached her that Anne, much influenced by the charismatic Queen Henrietta Maria, and a priest, who went by the names of both Johnson and Terret, was threatening to convert to Catholicism and wished to become a nun. Anna was able to stay only briefly with her daughters before she was obliged to go to Scotland, which she reached in May 1660. She must have been greatly excited at the thought of seeing her sons. Perhaps she also felt nervous as to how the two little boys, whom she had left when the youngest was only an infant, would react at the sight of the mother, who to them was almost a stranger, if indeed even the eldest remembered her at all. It seems that she need not have worried. The Reverend Mr Forret had cared for them as if they had been his own children despite the difficulties involved. Their father, before leaving Scotland on that winter's day seven year before, had made, as he thought, secure financial arrangements for their needs, but, as has already been told, when his estate was forfeited, all funding ceased.[5] Most probably Forret's wife, or his house-keeper, made the boys' clothes from homespun and woven wool. Certainly, somehow, the worthy minister had not only clothed and fed them but had given them the rudiments of education and religious instruction. The two boys, Charles and Colin, were sturdy little chaps, who, in the words of Lord Lindsay, 'like wild flowers on the Craig of Balcarres, lived and throve in the "caller air" of the north.'[6] Presented now to their mother, their faces scrubbed, their hair well-brushed, and dressed in their best clothes, they must have gazed in amazement at this tall and elegant woman with her still-lovely auburn hair and swirling skirts, who dropped on her knees to hold out her arms to them, her two, long-lost little boys.

Countess Anna is known to have been at Balcarres by Thursday, 17 May 1660, for on that day she wrote to her cousin, Lord Lauderdale, now thankfully nearing the end of his long imprisonment in the Tower: 'I bless the Lord for it, I have here two of the prettiest, healthfulest boys that can be, and so like their dear father that I know not which of them be said is the lykest.'[7]

The castle of Balcarres, no longer sequestered by the state, had changed little since that day in the winter of 1653 when Anna had left for France with her husband and daughters. During their absence, in fact, the house seemed to have been preserved in a timewarp for nothing was changed. The turnpike stair still led to their bedroom, with its low ceiling and linenfold panelled walls. Their clothes still hung in the presses and Balcarres' books stood in neat rows in the library where he and his cousin John Lauderdale had discussed their literary merits with Anna acting as mediator when their arguments became too heated. Close by was the great hall, or dining room where Anna, then heavily pregnant, had entertained the nineteen-year-old Charles II. How clearly she must have remembered that banquet in the February of 1651. Perhaps, in the now-empty, silent room, she could even recall the voices and laughter and in her mind's eye picture the flushed, excited faces of men rising from the table to toast the monarch, who was as young as most of them.

The fortunes of the Balcarreses had then seemed at their zenith. It was just over a month since the king, at his coronation at Scone, had given Alexander an earldom, made him Secretary of State, and hereditary governor of Edinburgh Castle and named him as High Commissioner of the General Assembly of the Kirk, destined to meet at St Andrews in the following July.

That night the room had been bright with firelight and from candles flaming in the sconces on the walls. Now, although fires had been lit in the long-unused rooms, hastily swept and dusted, the house, with all its memories, seemed claustrophobic and cold. She must have been thankful to escape from its confinement into the open air of the garden where the rooks still cawed and nested in the upper branches of the old elms. The New Plantation, which she and Alexander had planted when they were first married, had grown from saplings into trees. Also, most probably, weeds now smothered the flower-beds which Anna had made round the house.

These things, however, seemed of small importance to Anna as she and her sons scrambled up to the top of the Craig of Balcarres, then bare of trees and laurels, to gaze at the panoramic view. Again one can picture the three of them, the little boys breathless with excitement, pointing out the familiar landmarks to their newly returned mama. There in the foreground were the village kirk and the storeyed tower of the castle standing out against the vivid background of the sea. Then looking across to the south shore of the Firth of Forth the unmistakable outline of the Bass Rock, jutting upwards to the sky, with behind it, on the mainland, the pyramid shape of North Berwick Law immediately catching the eye. Still further away the distant gleam of Edinburgh shone out against the dark, distinctive outline of Arthur's Seat.

*

Following his return to England Charles II restored Episcopacy as the established religion of Scotland. Nonetheless, despite the Royal decree, Countess Anna remained a devout Presbyterian as did several other great ladies in the land. Amongst them the Duchess of Hamilton and the Countess (later to be the Duchess) of Rothes openly supported the Covenanters.

Indeed Anne, Duchess of Rothes, a daughter of Lord Crawford-Lindsay, is known to have hidden nonconformist preachers in the woods round her husband's castle of Leslie. 'A quiet understanding' existed between husband and wife. When forced, for the sake of appearance, to order a search for the rebellious ministers, the duke would murmur 'My hawks will be out tonight my Lady – take care of your blackbirds!' and with that she would hang a white sheet on a tree on the hill behind the castle, which could be seen for miles.[8]

*

Twelve days after Countess Anna's arrival at Balcarres, on Tuesday, 29 May 1660, the king, who had landed at Dover four days earlier, entered London to scenes of wild rejoicing.

It was exactly two weeks after this, on Friday, 12 June, that Anna Balcarres with her two little sons finally buried her husband, their father, in the family chapel at Balcarres. How she must have remembered the day, almost twenty years before, when, as a girl of just eighteen, she had come as his bride to the castle. Alexander, himself then only twenty-two, had been heir to a prosperous estate. Deeply in love with each other, life had held such promise for them both. Little could they have even guessed at the tragedies and troubles which, in those early days of their marriage, lay like a dark cloud beyond the horizon, invisible and unimaginable except to a few people like their uncle by marriage, the first Lord Lauderdale, who had guessed at what lay ahead.

Countess Anna spent a bare two months at Balcarres before the utter confusion of her financial position forced her to return to London. This time she took the boys with her on what was either a long journey by land, or more probably a shorter one by sea. We do not know where she lived in London. She did not own a house there so must have taken lodgings, most likely in one of the less fashionable areas of the city due to her lack of funds. The best houses then were in Whitehall and Pall Mall, from where it was easy to stroll and mix with society in St James's Park. Later her son Colin, having fortunately married an heiress, was to have a good lodging in the end of a street next to Whitehall.[9] Meanwhile, in the heat of the London summer of 1660, his mother had to put up with something more humble, unbecoming to her state. Nevertheless, even threadbare carpets, cheap furniture and the lack of her own carriage were of small importance compared with the joy of having her daughters returned to her once more: Anne, verging on womanhood, preoccupied with religion, Henrietta, a nervous, introverted girl of about fourteen and Sophia, a precocious eleven-year-old, arrived from Holland. Someone, possibly Princess Mary of Orange, had lent them or even given them the money for their passage across the North Sea.

The travellers reached London to find the city in a buzz of excitement over the arrest of the Marquess of Argyll. Argyll, who was owed no less than £40,000 by the Treasury, had been warned by his son, Lord Lorne, that the king, believing him to have conspired towards his father's execution, disliked him intensely. Nonetheless, he insisted on going to Whitehall to swear loyalty to the monarch on whose head, ten years before at Scone, he had set the crown.

Arriving at the Palace of Whitehall he was told by the Lord Chancellor, the Earl of Clarendon, that the king would not even receive him. Arrested by the Garter King of Arms in full public view, he was promptly confined to the Tower. There he remained for five months until, on 7 December, he was sent by sea to Scotland to be imprisoned in Edinburgh Castle. Then in February, in Parliament House, with General Middleton as Royal Commissioner, he stood trial on a charge of treason. Convicted on the evidence of letters written to General Monck and Colonel Lilburne during the Glencairn Rising, which proved his collaboration with the English regime, Argyll was executed by the 'Maiden', the Scots guillotine, on Monday, 27 May 1661.

All that is known of Countess Anna at this time is that, living in London, she was constantly struggling to find enough money to exist. Sir Robert Murray, in his letter to Alexander Bruce, had already expressed his great concern as to what would happen.[10] King Charles, in his letter of 29 March, had promised to help her as soon as he could. That he meant to do so is proved by a letter she wrote to Sir Edward Hyde, now the Earl of Clarendon and Lord High Chancellor of England.

Clarendon, surprisingly in view of the fact that he had been her husband's inveterate enemy, had been kind to her after Alexander's death. Anna, in a letter forwarded to him by Lord Lauderdale, wrote: 'I shall only just put you in mind that I rely confidently upon the assurance I gathered from your favourable expressions concerning my desires and his Majesty's gracious promises, and earnestly beg your Lordship may be pleased to interpose your credit with him again to make them effectual.'[11]

Sadly, the king himself was burdened with a chronic lack of money. In August, three months after his restoration, he is known to have said to an acquaintance, 'I must tell you I am not richer, that is, I have not so much money in my purse as when I came to you.'[12]

Countess Anna did eventually receive a pension but, even two years later, in 1662, in a letter to Lauderdale, then Secretary of State for Scotland, she said 'I am not for the present mistress of sixpence.'[13]

Most of what is known about Lady Balcarres at this time comes from the pen of Richard Baxter, who mentions her so frequently in his memoirs and other writings that, reading between the lines, one senses he was in love with her. Countess Anna, still only forty, was a striking and beautiful woman. Moreover she had an intellectual ability unusual for one, even of high rank, in those times.

Baxter came to know her through a friendship with Lord Lauderdale who, when a prisoner in Portsmouth and in

Windsor Castle, with much time on his hands, discovered his books. The best-known of these, 'The Saint's Rest', appealed to him so greatly that he read and took notes of all the others Baxter had written. So much was he impressed with them that 'he earnestly recommended them to Lord Balcarres and the king'.

What the king thought of them we do not know but Alexander Balcarres, having glanced through them, thought that he spoke 'too favourably of the papists and differed from many other Protestants, and so cast them by'. He then wrote to Lauderdale to tell him what he thought of them – rubbish in so many words, but Lauderdale 'pressed him to read one of the books through, which he did, and so read them all'. Anna, on her husband's recommendation, then read them as well and as a result became, as Baxter himself said, 'a most affectionate friend to me before she ever saw me'.[14] They finally did meet when she was in London in the winter of 1660–61.

Baxter's admiration for Anna, amounting almost to idolisation, reveals itself when he writes:

> Her great wisdom, modesty, piety, and sincerity made her accounted the saint at the court . . . She is of a solid understanding in religion for her sex, and of prudence much more than ordinary, and of great integrity and constancy in her religion, and a great hater of hypocrisy, and faithful to Christ in an unfaithful world . . . Being my constant auditor and ever respectful friend, I had occasion for the just praises and acknowledgments which I have given her.'[15]

Now, at the end of 1660, Baxter was to involve himself in a family matter, as Anne, Countess Anna's eldest daughter, defied her mother in her determination to become a Roman Catholic. Anna and her eldest daughter had for some time been at variance, possibly because they were too alike. Both had strong religious convictions. Neither was prepared to compromise and certainly not to give in. Lady Anne, a very pious girl, writing to her mother told her that she had 'made it her whole business till seventeen years of age to pray to God to direct her to follow his doctrine'.[16] Obsessed with religion, she was, as noted earlier, very susceptible to the dynamic influence of Queen Henrietta Maria and the plausible Jesuit priests favoured at the queen's court. Lord Lindsay believed that these people took advantage of Anna's visit to Scotland to entrap Anne, who was emotionally disturbed, having just lost her father.

This, to her mother, was anathema. Raised as a Scottish Episcopalian, she had later, together with her husband, adhered with great conviction to the Presbyterian Church of Scotland. In desperation she appealed to Doctor Gunning, one of the leading British clergymen, who was later to become the Bishop of Chichester. She begged him to talk, first to the mysterious and rather sinister priest, who was called both Johnson and Terret at different times and then, having done so, to try to convince Anne of how she had been misled.

But Dr Gunning, however well meaning, succeeded only in making things worse. He began, as Baxter wrote, 'to persuade her daughter against the Church of Scotland which she had been bred in as no true church, and afterwards disputed but about the Pope's infallibility'. What, in fact, he was trying to do was to convince her that 'the sure footing she sought for amid the diversities of theological opinion and private judgment which she observed among the Protestants could only be found in the Apostolical doctrine of the Catholic Church as represented by the Reformed Church of England'.[17] He might as well have saved his breath for Lady Anne, confused by his complicated arguments, but nonetheless probably aware that he was trying to make her join the Church of England, clung with obstinate, and for a girl of seventeen with admirable tenacity, to the decision she had already made.

Then came Mr Baxter, who found Countess Anna physically ill, worn out with misery and worry. At her behest he tried repeatedly to persuade the mysterious priest to meet him and to discuss the claims of Rome with Anne and himself. This he failed to achieve. The priest would not be coerced. He knew, it seems, that he had won.

Lady Anne was kidnapped, 'stolen away secretly from her mother in a coach, conveyed to France and put into a nunnery', where, Baxter added in his later accounts, not without a touch of malice, 'she is since dead'.[18]

In fairness to Anne, she may not have realised how her conversion to Catholicism and her disappearance, which she may have helped to arrange, would affect her mother.

She did in fact write to her soon after she arrived in France, when, having explained the reasons for her conversion, she signed herself 'Sister Anna Maria'.

It was Baxter who answered, because Countess Anna, exhausted both physically and mentally, was now extremely ill. Furious at her treatment by what he obviously thought was a heartless girl, he poured out a diatribe which must only have hardened her resolve. 'We shall have leave to pray for you, though we cannot have leave to instruct you; and God may hear us when you will not; which I have the more hopes of because of the piety or your parents, and the prayers and tears of a tender mother poured out for you.'[19]

*

Countess Anna for her part seems to have accepted that nothing she or anyone else could do would bring Anne back. Resigning herself to losing her she spent the whole of the next year of 1661 in London trying to obtain enough money for herself and her remaining children to live on, and also to prevent the mortgagers from reclaiming Balcarres' estate. Her pension, promised by the king, was at last paid in small instalments but she was still so badly off that she decided to return to Scotland where she could at least live off the farm produce which the tenants paid partly in rent. Accordingly she sent the two little boys, Charles and Colin, off to Balcarres Castle at the beginning of 1662 and followed with the two remaining girls, Henrietta and Sophia, the following May.

Before she left she asked Baxter to preach the last sermon she was to hear from him. His text was the words of Christ. 'Behold, the hour cometh, yea, is now come, that ye shall be scattered every one to his own, and shall leave me alone; and yet I am not alone, because the father is with me.' She had need, as he said, 'for all the consolation such thoughts could give her'[20], for soon, in addition to her constant financial problems, she was to have to endure yet another even more terrible anxiety over the increasing illness of Charles, now since his father's death, the 2nd Earl of Balcarres, her eldest son.

'For God's Sake Do All That You Can'

———>►●◄———

Anna Balcarres, now seriously in debt, wrote to Lord Lauderdale asking for both help and advice. Hurtful to her pride as this must have been, it was the sensible and obvious answer to her predicament for none was better placed to help her than Lauderdale, by then in high favour with the king.

John Maitland, 2nd Earl of Lauderdale, her first cousin (their mothers, daughters of Lord Dunfermline, being sisters) was himself no stranger to adversity. Born in 1616, he had, in 1647, been commissioned by the Scottish parliament to treat with King Charles I at Hampton Court. The result had been the raising of an army to restore the king. Later, sent to Holland to treat with Charles II, he had returned with him to Scotland in 1650.

Subsequently, together with the Duke of Hamilton, he had at first lain low for fear of the disfavour of the Marquess of Argyll, then omnipotent. Shortly afterwards, however, he had won great favour with the king, who famously described him as the only Scotsman he liked.

Charles' liking for him is, at first glance, hard to understand for, unlike the monarch himself, Maitland was not a handsome man. With sprouting locks of red hair falling to his collar, framing his narrow face, he has been described as a grotesque figure, reminiscent of Shakespeare's Caliban. Nonetheless he was a forceful character, both witty and, when he turned it on, possessed of a captivating charm. The king, who loved to be amused, enjoyed his clever turn of phrase. Also, he believed him to be unshakeably loyal.

Captured at Worcester, Lauderdale had endured nine years of imprisonment, some of them in a darkened dungeon, during Cromwell's rule. Following the Restoration he had been richly rewarded. Created Secretary of State for Scotland and President of the Council, in addition to other appointments, he was now the most influential man in Scotland. In England he was amongst a group of nobles, headed by the Duke of Buckingham, who were conniving at Clarendon's fall from power.

*

Countess Anna wrote to Lord Lauderdale, on 4 July 1662, shortly after her return to Balcarres. Asking him to show her letter to the king, she said, 'and for God's sake do all you can to get me a speedy answer'. She was trying to twist the king's arm to get his High Treasurer, Lord Crawford-Lindsay, to release some of the money that had been promised to her. Telling Lauderdale, 'I am not for the present mistress of sixpence', she then adds magnanimously, but with a touch of sarcasm:

Yet I will not blame my Lord Crawford, how ill soever he use me. I am rather sorry he is so unfortunate never to oblige his friends and those that wish him best. I would beseech your Lordship to speak to him, not as from me but from yourself – desire that he would let me have presently but that money there is in precepts (orders) drawn for, which is two hunder and fifty pound [that] my Lord Ballantyne [Bellenden] drew, and a hunder that rest unpaid of the two hundred and fifty pounds gave for me before he left Scotland. If he would cause presently to give me the three hundred and fifty pounds, or four hundred pounds, it would pay all what I owe yet at London and do some necessary things I have to do here. I owe to Mr Dudney a hundred pounds, which Sir William Waller is bound for, that must be precisely paid the beginning of August, and a hundred pounds to Mrs Tyler my Lord Crawford is bound for himself – besides all my apothecary's accompts and others there, as Mr Drummond can tell you, will be more than sixty pound . . . O me! My dear Lord, think upon the complications of afflictions I have to go under; my pressures, and the apprehensions I have and disturbance for my poor child Charles, are not easy to bear.[1]

This is the first mention of Charles's illness, although reference to the apothecary's bills suggests that she had been spending much money on medicines. Countess Anna herself was now again so ill that the good Mr Forret, who had been guardian of her two sons, took it upon himself, unbeknown to Anna, to write to Lord Lauderdale of the family's desperate plight.

It is easy to picture the kind old gentleman in his study, wearing the black clothes of his calling, his wig upon his head, sharpening the point of his plume with care before dipping it into the ink-well to begin, in his copperplate hand, to write to one of the most powerful men in the kingdom, whom perhaps he may have known as a boy, to describe the plight of the family whose troubles he felt as his own:

Right Honourable,

My Lady Balcarres some hours after she sent her servant for London fell in a very sore and most dangerous fit of sickness. Mr Wood was present with her all that night; he told me her weakness was so great (her pulse for some hours not being discernible) that he looked every moment for present death. The next day I went into the town and found my lady in a condition little better; and therefore we resolved presently to send to Sir John Wedderburn for his advice. Mr Wood (who has some skill in medicine) sent an information

97

to the doctor concerning her disease . . . My lady after the fourth night (blessed be God!) became some better, but is still very weak and oppressed with extreme grief, whilk she keeps within, not making it known to any save me, whom my lady knows to be fully acquainted with the cause of it.

The present great straits my lady is in, the difficulty which she hath to provide for her family, though she live as frugally and sparingly as any can do, the clear foresight she hath of the inevitable ruin of the estate if the Lord in mercy do not prevent it, do so overwhelm her spirit that her stomach is near gone; and [she] gets very little sleep in the night; and such a weak body as my lady hath cannot long subsist in this condition. If my Lord Crawford knew but half so much of my lady's straits as I do, I am persuaded he would not be so forgetful of her as he is. It is no wonder that my lady is in such straits, and hath such difficulty in maintaining her family, seeing the rent of her jointure for the year 1662 was all spent before my lady came to Scotland. A part of it was detained in the tenants' hands for money previously advanced by them; a considerable part of it was sent by bill to London for bringing home the children, and the rest spent in the house before my lady's return; so that all this last summer (in which time my lady was at great charges, partly by physicians and partly by going several times to Edinburgh about her necessary affairs) my lady was necessitated to live on the rent of her jointure for the crop of 1662; and now that year's rent is wholly exhausted, and verily my lady is in such perplexity that she knows not whither to turn.

There is no money here for borrowing. My lady's tenants can do no more for her help than they have done, so that if the Treasurer do not for her, I profess seriously I see no other of it but that within a few weeks she shall be reduced to as great extremity as ever she was when she lived among strangers.

And therefore, my noble Lord, I must so far presume as humbly and with all earnestness to entreat your Honour, for the Lord's sake, and as ye tender the life of your dear friend, to deal effectually with my Lord Crawford for a considerable and present supply; for her condition admits of no delay. As for the estate, it is in a most desperate condition, if something is not done by his Majesty for the recovery of it, it is ruined.

Your Lordship, I am confident, will do in this what possibly can be done; and whenever any grounds of hope appear that anything can be done for preserving it from ruin, if your Honour shall be pleased to make this known to my lady, it would much revive her, and ease her of that burden of grief that weighs down her heart.

I add no more, but humbly craving pardon for the trouble I put your Honour to by this too long letter, I shall always continue,

My noble Lord,
Your Lordship's most humble servant,
Mr David Forret.[2]

Mr Forret's letter, combined with Anna's own, must have influenced Lord Lauderdale to approach Lord Crawford-Lindsay, the High Treasurer, for the money owed to Anna, at first in small instalments, was eventually paid.

In the meantime the dread of what appeared to be inevitable bankruptcy was overshadowed by a still greater fear as Anna's eldest son became fatally ill. She poured out her heart to Lauderdale as she described his last days. 'This child has had like a quotidian ague since April last; till within this two month, six weeks ago [he continued] to have his own fresh colour and flesh – ten days before God took him he became very melancholy and did sensibly decay daily; his clear colour became blackish, and his hands and feet seldom or never hot.'

She continued to describe how, on the Sunday before he

died, she would not let him go to church. Nonetheless he had spent the day in reading and praying, and although he had no music, in singing psalms. The last psalm he sang being the final part of the 34th. For the next two days he had been terribly sick and had a most sad sigh,

which made me question him what made him sigh so deeply. He said he had many challenges that he had not spent his time so in the service of God as he should have done, he was in some anxiety of spirit for an hour, but after he had prayed and given himself up to God, and cast all his burden upon his Mediator and Cautioner, he was at great quiet, said he had not the least trouble to leave the world, only to leave 'his dear lady mother and Sophia'. Upon Wednesday morning, at six o'clock, after a quiet night's rest, in a moment he found all his strength and spirits decay together, and called to me, and threw his arms about my neck, and prayed God to 'bless his dear lady mother', desired Mr Forret to pray, and then he looked up and desired of God that the blood of Jesus Christ would clean him of all his sins, and that He would take him to be for ever with Himself, which He immediately did – so my dear child went to Him that made him without either pain or sickness.

I caused open him – his lungs and all his noble parts was untouched; he had a great liver and a great spleen full of black blood, yet had no blood at all in his veins; only his heart was his defect, which had in it a stone which weighs an ounce and a half. The stone and the physician's description that opened him I intend to send to your Lordship to let Dr Fraser see, who I know will be troubled for his father's son, and will give me his advice concerning the rest of my poor children, who are now a small number – but blessed be the Lord for what I have! He gives and he takes.[3]

Countess Anna's acceptance of yet another tragedy typifies the devout belief of so many of her time when the death of children was so common that in some families none survived. In the light of modern medicine Charles would appear to have died from chronic heart disease. The 'quotidian ague' which his mother mentions was probably rheumatic fever, which often results in aortic heart disease, the aortic valve becoming so calcified that it could be taken for a stone. Inevitably this would have resulted in the failure of the left-hand side of his heart. The Dr Fraser she mentions was Sir Alexander Fraser, Court Physician to Charles II, and a great friend of both Lord Lauderdale and her brother-in-law Sir Robert Moray, who were at that time in London. She did in fact get Archbishop Sharp of St Andrews to take 'the stone' which had been found in Charles' heart to London, together with another letter to Lauderdale in which she says, pathetically: 'My Lord, pray let me know what physicians say of it, and if there could have been help for it, and whether they think he had it from his conception, or but lately grown.'[4]

Charles' illness, while so distressing to his mother and sisters, was also a cause of great expense. That doctors charged large fees is proved by Anna's household accounts of a later date, which show that she paid out no less than £48 for their attendance in one year alone. Meanwhile, in 1662, as Charles lay so desperately ill, his mother, although greatly in debt, was so frantic to save him that she somehow managed to find or borrow enough money to pay the best physicians that could be found.

As when she herself was ill, it is likely that Charles was first attended by Mr Wood, who 'with some skill in medicine' may have been the local doctor. However, under the circumstances it seems probable that the eminent Sir John Wedderburn, a specialist in Edinburgh called in to give a second opinion on Anna's own illness, was also summoned to the bedside of her son. Sadly, in this case, neither he nor anyone else could do more than use opiates to try to alleviate the suffering of the boy who, only three years before, on her return to Scotland, had run so joyously into his mother's arms.

On 21 October 1662, six days after his death, Charles, 2nd Earl of Balcarres, aged just twelve years and eight months, was buried in the family chapel of his home. As was then the custom with the interment of women and children, the service was held at night. Lord Lindsay describes the 'the sepulchral edifice, with its Gothic arches, armorial insignia and mortuary carvings lit up by torches, and the mourning groups of kindred and vassals committing to the dust the tender flower which had so recently been blooming among them'.[5]

Mr Forret conducted the funeral service of the boy who for nine years had been as a son to him while his parents were forced to live abroad. Charles in his twelve years had known his mother for a bare four. His father, whom he dimly remembered, only for two. The short life of the second Lord Balcarres had been blighted, like those of so many other children in Scotland, by the evils of civil war.

CHAPTER 12

'I Can Bear Another's Unkindness
Rather Than Your Silence'

Countess Anna's correspondence with Lord Lauderdale reveals her constant worry over money. In particular she asked him to enquire about the pension which the king, despite his promises, still failed to produce. On his failing to answer a letter she had sent him describing her son's death, she was obviously hurt by his neglect. Her letter is lodged amongst the Lauderdale papers in the British Museum but, believing that the messenger she had sent had not delivered it (he seems to have been in some sort of mishap on the voyage to London) she wrote again on 24 February 1663:

My Lord,

I wrote to your Lordship not long ago a long letter of all that concerns me, and it's lost by the misfortune this poor boy had by sea: yet I resolved to send him again that I may by him hear from your Lordship, and also let you know all the difficulties and straits I am put to by reason of the debt contracted in England, Holland and when I was last in Scotland, which is almost all to pay yet. Here I must again tell your Lordship that my Lord Kellie told me that which vexed me, which was that your Lordship had neither had mine, wherein I gave you an account of my dear child's sickness and death, wherein I enclosed some epitaphs made upon him.

So long as it is in my mind I must break off saying somewhat like thanks, and tell you, though I will not the least quarrel, that I think it a very long time since I heard from your Lordship, and can bear another's unkindness better than your silence . . .

I would let you know that I got none of my pension, which I believe you know not; and if my difficulties and straits and burdens is become too heavy for my estate and, I may say for my heart to bear, had I not got a good and tender-hearted reconciled God to go to, I could not but succumb . . . I have said somewhat to my Lord Treasurer, whose absence is, I know prejudicial to me. I should be glad if your Lordship would agree for a sure pension to me with the Treasurer, so I give down two or three hundred pounds. Your Lordship do in this as you please. I pray you, my Lord, let me hear from you. The Lord of Heaven and Earth be with you, and bless, direct and protect you, is the prayer of

Your most affectionate cousin and humble servant
Anne Balcarres

Pray, my Lord, forgive the writ of this; for the whole grammar-school almost was in the hall, and I knew hardly for their noise what I was writing.[1]

From this it seems that Countess Anna was then living in St Andrews for the benefit of her youngest child's education. Colin, now aged eleven, had apparently invited some of his schoolmates to their house and, like most boys of their age, when let out of school, they were happily letting off steam. By the mid-sixteenth century, while most villages in Fife had schools, grammar schools existed only in the towns.[2] Alexander Balcarres had been educated at Haddington Grammar School, where another former pupil had been John Knox. Therefore it seems likely that Colin, following in his father's footsteps, precious only son as he now was, was sent to St Andrews because it was closer to home.

Lord Lauderdale must have replied to Anna's letter for, on 11 April she wrote again:

My dear Lord,

Yours did most exceedingly satisfy me. How unfortunate soever I may appear to myself in many things, yet I shall never think I am really so long as God Almighty give me my best friends, and that they are well and not changed to me . . . I confess my melancholy made me a little jealous you had a little forgot me; but pray, my dear Lord, forgive me all my faults and I shall easily forgive you all yours I did quarrel with you for, so you will let me hear but once a month from you, were it but three words, not a full line – I am well and as you wish me. I pray the Lord bless, direct and have a care of you; for so wishes she with all her heart, who is, my dear Lord,

Your most affectionate servant

Anne Balcarres

I sent the physician's paper [the report concerning her son Charles's illness] once to your Lordship already, which you desire. I have sent to him for another; if it come in time I shall enclose it here; if it come not my Lady Rothes will convey it to your Lordship. Pray, my Lord, convey my kindest respects to my Lady and my Lady Mary, and Lady Lorn.[3]

Lauderdale had married Anne, daughter of Earl Howe; their only child was the Lady Mary to whom Anna sent her good wishes. Her mention of Lady Lorn (sic) is significant in that it suggests a continuing friendship between Anna and Lord and Lady Lorne. The highly excitable Lord Lorne, who had quarrelled so violently with MacDonnell of Glengarry and with Lord Glencairn in the Royalist camp at Lochaber, had married Lady Mary Stuart, eldest daughter of the 4th Earl of Moray. A brave and devoted wife, she seems to have calmed him down. In 1663, when Anna mentions her name, her husband was just about to be restored as the 9th Earl of Argyll by Charles II. The marquisate, however, granted to his father by Charles I, but forfeited after the Marquess's execution, was never to be regained.

These letters provide the main information of Anna's troubles and of her continuing financial worries following her husband's death. It is only towards the end of 1663 that there seems to be a glimmer of hope that some money might be available. On 16 November 1663, Anna wrote again to Lord Lauderdale, enclosing another to the king, reminding him that some time previously he had promised her the value of the fine imposed upon Sir James MacDonald. Sir James MacDonald of Dunyveg, with great estates in both the island of Islay and the mainland of Kintyre, had been forfeited of his lands after the defeat of his rising against the government of James VI & I in 1615. The income of his former property, once held by the Crown, had been held in the Treasury of the Scottish Parliament. King Charles II's promise to Countess Anna, therefore, must have been based on his knowledge of this fund. In the letter to Lord Lauderdale she wrote:

My Lord

According to your advice I have written to his Majesty in general of my condition, having left the particulars to be [by] your Lordship represented to him, which are, if you would please to desire his Majesty out of the fines to grant me the value of Sir James MacDonald's fine, which was £5,000, which he promised me, without which your Lordship knows what a deplorable condition this estate and family is in; and that, for the better payment of my pension, you would desire his Majesty to let it be either drawn upon the excise, or some locality appointed me; but, if none of this be feasible, that his Majesty would write a letter to the Exchequer according to your own effectual wording of it, that it may be surely paid.

Some makes me to believe, that if your Lordship do not somewhat to secure me, it will be but little worth. I confess I listened to what they said with the more dread that, when you was in Scotland, I could not prevail at my earnest desire, to get £70 when I was in so great a strait as it forced me to leave all my writs here and there, as we say, for want of money, and yet am not able to relieve them . . . Most of this year's rent I was forced to spend. I have not [wherewithal] to pay my servant's wages, nor my house I had at St Andrews, nor to keep my son there.

My Lord, I will say no more, knowing the way you will take will be that you think most for my advantage, according to the entire confidence I have in your love and kindness to my Lord,

Your affectionate Cousin

and humble servant,

Anne Balcarres

Pray my dear Lord, present my most humble service to my Lady and my Lady Mary. I have not had a word from my Lord Treasurer [Lord Crawford-Lindsay] since I saw you. I pray, my Lord, seal this [i.e. the enclosed letter] with a common seal – none of your known inscriptions.[4]

This letter, with its reference to the young Earl Colin, seems to have struck a chord in Lord Lauderdale's heart, for about two months later he sent him his first sword as the gift of a kinsman. Colin, absolutely delighted, wrote, in his school-boy's hand, to thank him for this gift, of which he was obviously very proud.

Balcarres, 23rd Jan 1664

My Lord

I have with no small contentment girded your Lordship's present to my side, and I shall use it in my Sovereign's and your service; for, if by his Royal bounty and your Lordship's endeavours I be not prevented, the law will not suffer me to employ it in the defence of any such thing as I might call an inheritance. I do therefore with thankfulness embrace your sword as an addition to your former favours and an earnest of your future care of, my Lord,

Your Lordship's most humble and obliged servant,
Balcarres[5]

Lord Lauderdale, stirred by the appeal of Countess Anna's letter, did more than send the present of his prized first sword to her son. On 13 February 1664, a royal mandate was issued. Addressed to Lord Rothes, who had succeeded his father-in-law Lord Crawford-Lindsay as Treasurer, it directed that Lady Balcarres' and other pensions (payment of which had hitherto, it is stated, been restricted to one half only of what was due) should henceforward be paid 'completely'. As a result of this it appears she did at least get enough money to settle her outstanding bills, although payment in full was delayed for at least two years owing to the Exchequer itself being drained dry of funds.

On 28 March (old style) 1664, Countess Anna wrote a long letter to a Madam Henderson, herself recently a widow, who was another member of the Fordell family with whom the Balcarreses kept in close touch. It appears that this lady had not only helped her financially but had arranged the shipment of some of Anna's possessions from Holland:

Madam, I have received my beds and books, and also what you was at the pains to pay for me. The three porcelain pots

I like very well; they come safe. So did the other twenty pots, but they were all empty. I had some hope your ladyship should have procured some flowers from Madame Sommerdyke, and those that had gardens. I was so liberal when I had abundance, makes me have the fewer now. If there be any of the little money left your Ladyship did me the favour to cause buy these things with, bestow it all upon some plain cold gilded leather – those kind that were plain, as I remember, was not so dear as was the wrought leather; they were 28st [stivers] the piece. I know, if you have any money, it will buy but few.

Dear Madame, fail not in your promise to send me Monsieur Henderson and your picture, if you have them by you. I am sorry to put you to expense for me, though I desire them as much as can do anything. Coronell Henderson told me he had spoke to his sister, Madame Stencalven, for her picture to me, and told her that I desired it, and he said she promised to send it to him to send me. I pray you Madame, write to her of it, that I shall still make it my desire, and will think it a great favour if she will send it to me. She had let them have it that has not such relation to her as this family has.

I saw all my friends in Kellie, they are all very well, I thank God; and my good lady is the best woman in the world; she is so sweet an humour that we think ourselves happy in her; and my Lord and she loves each other so much that they are both wonderfully happy in each other.

It's time now I should make an end, so I will say no more but entreat you to believe I am unalterably, Dear Madam,

Your ladyship's affectionate cousin and humble servant,
Anne Balcarres

Pray Madam, do me the favour to present my kind respects to Madame Sommerdyck and her daughter, the Countess of Kincardine. I wonder I have not heard from none of them. If Madame Sommerdyck will not let me have my pictures, I shall think she thinks me not worth so great a favour. My blessing to your sweet child.[6]

Almost a year passed before, on the last day of February 1665, the Treasurer, Lord Rothes wrote to Lord Lauderdale to tell him of an advance towards a settlement of the long-pending Seaforth claims: 'For news, my Lady Balcarres and my Lord Seaforth are agreed, and I think, in all, better secured than ever.'[7]

Nonetheless it was still some time before the final settlement took place. Part of the arrangement made eventually was that the share of the fines made upon Cromwell's supporters in Scotland that were due to Seaforth would instead be bequeathed to Lady Balcarres.

Anna meanwhile, on 11 April, wrote again to Lord Lauderdale, cousin, both of herself and her husband, who once had been their closest friend:

My dear Lord,

I did once in my life scarce suppose, if living where within five days I might hear from you, that two years should run on without receiving a line from you. This your silence I am loathe to impune to forgetfulness, unkindness, or any bad impression of me, others have endeavoured to put upon you, but rather to your owing me as one of your own, and to the multitude and greatness of your affairs, and your being unwilling, as some others has informed me, to write till some considerable business for me by your means had been done . . . it's true I have often longed to have heard from you, and would gladly have accepted the least line from you, that I might have satisfied my own fear of a chance in your affection, and have assured others who have marvelled at your seeming not-remembrance of me.[8]

Anna, at Balcarres, waiting in vain for at least some acknowledgment of her letter to the man with whom both she and Alexander had once been on such close terms, was then greatly alarmed by a rumour that the jointure, owed to her by another cousin, Lord Seaforth, would not, after all be paid.

My Lord,

I hear by one that is come from London that there is a list made [of those] that has a share in the fines and that my cousin Seaforth and I is only put out. I confess it was bad news to me, whose heart, alas! is too much pressed with the heavy burden of my poor fatherless children and most dreadful covetous creditors. Though I had great hopes of his Majesty's bounty to me, and now am made believe I only am left out, I shall say nothing . . . Whatever I suffered for him was my duty. I repent it not. I wish this family was as able to serve him as first. We want not good will. Nor can I think when I remember what I know his Majesty [to be] that he will still retain his wanted goodness to me, and do somewhat for me, now when I so much need it. My Lord, I do verily believe your Lordship did all you could for me . . .

My children are well, I bless God; they are all your servants.

Sophia is at Edinburgh, with my Lady Rothes. I would take it as an inestimable favour to hear from your Lordship.[9]

She wrote again on 9 August but still there was no reply. Suspecting then that 'evil tongues' had been influencing him against her she sent yet another letter on 9 October, this time telling him in plain language how much he had hurt her feelings by refusing to send even the briefest acknowledgment in reply to the letters, some of which at least he must have received, over the space of three years.

Anna's letters to Lord Lauderdale, revealing his contemptuous refusal to recognise her plight, which, although she tried to excuse it as being caused by pressure of work, provide a clear indication of how, by the time of her writing them, he was steadily and irrevocably becoming corrupted by power.

Balcarres, 9th October

My Lord,

The day was, it was a satisfaction to me to write to the Earl of Lauderdale, because he was pleased sometimes to say it was so to him; but now your Lordship interesting yourself so little for me and mine as not so much as to see your handwrit in three years, nor to find my way that you mind us, I cannot but fear my friendship has become a burden, and so, I confess, it is with some pain I give you this trouble. I have been often going to ask your Lordship if ever I did in the least offend you or did anything unworthy of the friendship you was once pleased to allow me.[10]

With this letter, or at least with the same messenger, was another from her son Colin, now the 3rd Earl of Balcarres, and, as Lord Lindsay writes, 'his mother's little champion of thirteen', which could not, I think, have been read without sympathy:

Oct 9th 1665

My Lord,

I know I have no merit of my own to make your Lordship do anything for me, so it must be merely your goodness make you have any care for me. I know, were I a man, I must take my sword in my hand, ane beggar; but that troubles me not so much as the trouble I see my mother in for me. If your Lordship will be so good as to remember me to the king's majesty, who, I hear, promised my mother somewhat,

which, if she get it, I will look upon as given to me. If God make me a man worthy to serve your Lordship, you shall find me dedicate myself to your service, next to that of my prince. I am more ways than one obliged to be, my Lord,
Your most humble servant,
Balcarres.[11]

Lauderdale, stirred perhaps by her son's epistle, did at last respond to Anna's letters. Irritated perhaps by her insistence, and determined to eschew responsibility, he told her to write a personal letter to the king setting out the details of all that she had been promised in settlement of her claims regarding the forfeiture of property in his cause. She did:

Balcarres, the 2nd March

May it please your Majesty,

I have had such large and frequent testimonies of your Majesty's gracious condescension and favour towards me at all times, I am encouraged at this time, amidst your Majesty's great affairs, humbly to make known to your Majesty my own and the distressed condition of this family. It is true, and I do humbly acknowledge, your Majesty, in consideration of our condition, was pleased to grant me an yearly pension, but of that I have still owing me £4,000. Your Majesty did likewise promise to me and I suppose to my Lord Chancellor of England, who was pleased to speak to your Majesty for me, that I should have the value of Sir James MacDonald's fine, which was £5,000, towards the repairing of this ruined estate, occasioned by the great debt lying thereon, contracted by my husband in carrying on of your Majesty's service, as my Lord Secretary can more particularly inform . . .[12]

This letter was accompanied by another, written to Lauderdale seventeen days later, on 19 March. The delay suggests that she was waiting for one of the couriers who carried letters on horseback, there being then no regular post. Having received his answer and realised that he was doing his best to help her by telling her to write directly to the king, she plainly regretted the outburst of resentment expressed in her previous screed and wrote him a long, friendly letter explaining her situation. She ended by saying: 'I thank the Lord God that yourself, and Lady, and my Lady Mary and family have been preserved in the late mortality.* That you may be kept from it and from all trouble is among the most earnest and hearty wishes of, my dear Lord, Your Lordship's affectionate servant, Anne Balcarres'.[13]

This was almost the last letter that Countess Anna exchanged with Lord Lauderdale. Soon they were to quarrel over an issue unconcerned with money but which caused a final estrangement between these cousins who had once been the greatest of friends. Lauderdale, however, did continue to take an interest in and to support the young Lord Balcarres.

Soon after what proved to be the end of her correspondence with Lauderdale, Anna's promised pension seems to have been paid in full. She was therefore no longer in constant financial difficulty but it was not until three years later, in 1669, that, in the words of Lord Lindsay, 'her long deferred rights, her provision from the Seaforth inheritance as bequeathed to her by her father, were finally accorded and made payable to her son Balcarres'[14]. By arrangements then entered into, and on the consideration of 5,000 merks paid down at once, Balcarres, under his mother's tutory and direction, agreed to surrender his father's acquired rights over the estate of Seaforth on the security of a series of bonds by which the chieftains of the MacKenzies, Lord Tarbat, the Lairds of Suddie, Reidcastle, Applecross, Gareloch, Coull, Hilton,

---

* The Great Plague of London in 1666.

Assynt and others, together with Sir John Urquhart of Cromarty, made themselves responsible for the payment by instalments of sums of money amounting to above 80,000 merks, in liquidation of his claims. A long course of anxiety was thus brought to a happy determination.

CHAPTER 13

Two Marriages and a Funeral

The last years of the 1660s were perhaps the most peaceful of Countess Anna's whole life. She was, however, far from idle for, now that she could afford it, she busied herself in putting the estate of Balcarres to rights. 'Fair Balcarres' sunward-sloping farms', although famed as some of the most productive land in the Neuk of Fife, had, nonetheless, been allowed to run to seed. Nothing had been spent on their maintenance since Anna and Alexander had gone to Holland, on the summons of Charles II, in 1653. Houses and farm-buildings had to be repaired, ground needed to be drained and fertilised with dung, some hedges had to be cut and others planted, and dykes round the enclosures rebuilt with stone.

Countess Anna, who had a good head for business, managed gradually to pay off her creditors thanks in part to her augmented income and also to the slowly increasing profits from the estate. Thus, her son Colin found himself still in possession of some of the best land in Fife.

Colin Balcarres was sixteen when, either in 1669 or 1670, his mother sent him down to London 'to pay his duty to the king'. If her accounts are anything to go by he must have gone well equipped. Written in her own hand, with a plume which shed blots of ink, and spelt to some extent phonetically, as was common at the time, they give a good indication of the cost of being properly dressed at court.

Shoes were an average price of £1 7/ a pair. A pair of

Anna, Countess of Balcarres – probably painted at the time of her marriage in 1640. Artist unknown. *Photographed by Brendan MacNeill, reproduced courtesy of Lord Crawford of Balcarres.*

ABOVE. Balcarres etching from a sketch of 1794. *Reproduced courtesy of Lord Crawford of Balcarres.*

RIGHT. Alexander, 1st Earl of Balcarres. *Reproduced courtesy of the Scottish National Portrait Gallery.*

LEFT. The Reverend Richard Baxter. After Robert White. *Photographed by Roy Summers.*

BELOW. Frontispiece of Richard Baxter's memoirs, bearing the signature of Anna Balcarres and (very faintly) that of her daughter Henrietta. *Photographed by Brendan MacNeill, reproduced courtesy of Lord Crawford of Balcarres.*

Argyll's Lodging in Stirling – The Drawing Room. *Roy Summers.*

The High Dining Room where James, Duke of York was entertained to dinner by the Earl and Countess of Argyll in February 1681. *Roy Summers.*

The High Dining Room showing the work of the Edinburgh artist David McBeath who decorated the wooden partition dividing the room from the stairs in 1675. *Roy Summers.*

The Laigh Hall, or Entrance Hall, which was also the dining room for the senior household servants. *Roy Summers.*

Brusselles 29 March 1660.

Madame, I hope you are so well persuaded
of my kindnesse to you, as to beleeve that there
can no misfortune happen to you, and I not
have my share in it, I assure you I am touched
at the losse you have had, and I hope ~~from~~ that
God will be pleased to put me into such a con=
=dition before it be long, as I may let you see
the care I intend to have of you and your children
and that you may depends of my being very truly
        Madame
                Your affectionate frinde

                Charles R

Letter to Anna, Countess of Balcarres, from King Charles II, dated from Brussels, 29 March 1660. *Reproduced courtesy of Lord Crawford of Balcarres and the National Library of Scotland.*

Letter from Anna, Countess of Balcarres, signing herself Anne, referring to the King's proposed assistance in 1660, thought to have been forwarded by Lauderdale to the Lord Chancellor Clarendon. *Reproduced courtesy of Lord Crawford of Balcarres and the National Library of Scotland.*

Paris VI octob.
1659

My lady belearis y haue writ to
my daughter to desire her too assu
-re you againe of her good intentions
for you: and from mee you may
bee confident that y shall not lett
anie occation passe where in y may
lett you see the estime y haue of
you and how y am with great
truth
My lady belearis

your very goode and
assured freind
henriette Marie R

Letter from Henrietta Maria, widow of Charles I and mother of Charles II, dated
October, 1659, saying that she had written to her daughter, the Princess of Orange,
asking her to help the Balcarres family in any possible way. Countess Anna was
subsequently made *gouvernante* to the little Prince of Orange who later became William
III. *Reproduced courtesy of Lord Crawford of Balcarres and the National Library of Scotland.*

Item Iuing to be 8 hand curchers to him selev 2 0

for his broanutin mrie and to thepoer 4 15

13   13   00

mor for cloth to behis briches ———— 4   19

to Iams monw head ———— 8   12

fer 4 pear of Glues 1   3

fo mr mcclens man 8   14 0

to mr Bela 0   18

for nhi oufens xē 1   4

for drogs ———— 2   1 0

to mr Burnet 14   10 0

for 2 pear of shaws 3   15 0

for two rings to mr mcquin Rob mes 8   8   0

for 4 els of stuf to be a cot 7   10 0

for blak Glues 0   5   6

for tabie and bukels 4   16 0

for Lyning ———— 1   4   0

for Glues ———— 0   2   0

to Iams tamson teler for him 3   3   0

for a nig from Sanders michell 0   0

Countess Anna's housekeeping list, possibly, because of the sums paid to doctors, dating from 1662, as her son Charles died in October that year.
Reproduced courtesy of Lord Crawford of Balcarres and the National Library of Scotland.

to the skull offesers ——— spay 0 14 0

to the skull befer 0 14 6

In mence in smals 3 pear ok ——— 5 18 6

to mr mcdens man ——— 0 14 0

for dying 10 Els of stuff to be Lords 3 14 0

fer 3 pear of stekens to him 2 19 0

for a pear of cars Glaues 0 7 0

tw a wret Capte bock 0 12 0

to Bel fer dresens his Cot 2 14 0

29 sepr to mr Burnet and on of the

Docters ——— 11 12 0

to ane other Docter 2 18 0

9 sep ter 2 pear of shaws 3 18 0

for Glaues ——— 0 8 0

for his 10 octr Bocts ——— 10 12 4

to a teler ——— 2 15 0

mor 18 oct 1 18 0

Giuen to mr Burnet and his dockers

14 10 0

to Glaues ——— 0 8 0

Portrait of William III to whom Countess Anna had been governess as a little boy.
Attributed to Sir Godfrey Kneller. *Reproduced courtesy of the National Galleries of Scotland.*

LEFT. Portrait of Charles II as a boy. William Dobson. *Reproduced courtesy of the National Galleries of Scotland.*

BELOW. Portrait of Archibald, 9th Earl of Argyll. *Reproduced courtesy of the National Galleries of Scotland.*

'stokens' (stockings) cost £1 16/ and three pairs of gloves 17/6. Mr John Campbell 'for furnishing a set of cloths' (clothes) charged no less than £30, the cloth for his briches alone amounting to £4 19/ while '4 els of stuff to be a cot' (coat) came to £7 16/, the lining at £1 4/ extra. More expensive still the lining of a red coat, amounting to '3 els and a half of body serg' cost £6 18/ and 'a silver frenge [fringe] to his westcoat', reached the exorbitant sum of £20. Other items included a wig supplied by Sanders Mitchel for 3 guineas and dancing shoes at £2 18/.

Thus, with much luggage and several attendants, did Colin Balcarres depart for London, a tremendous excitement for the boy, only just approaching manhood, who had only left Scotland once in his life before. Arriving in London, the young earl stayed with his uncle, Sir Robert Moray, who cared for him with paternal affection, and was presented to the king by Lord Lauderdale.

King Charles II, himself still a very handsome man, recognised Colin Balcarres at once by his great resemblance to his father. Now, as he knelt before him, he saw again the well-remembered manly figure, the auburn hair, and the good-looking open face. Moved by the recollection of how Alexander Balcarres had lost life and land for his cause, he exclaimed, with some emotion, that 'he had loved his father and would be a father to him himself'.[1] Then, in proof of his favour, he gave him the command of a select troop of horse, composed of 100 loyal gentlemen who had been reduced to poverty during the recent troubles, and who had half-a-crown a day as their military pay.[2]

King Charles was not the only one to be impressed by Balcarres' good looks. He seems to have made quite a stir amongst the ladies of the court. Proof of this came when, a few days after his presentation, he fell dangerously ill of a fever, no doubt contracted from the unhealthy atmosphere of the city, against which, as a country boy, he had no immunisation. Sir Robert, horrified, fearing he must tell Anna the worst, summoned physicians but, thanks to a good constitution, Colin survived their potions and bleeding and soon recovered his health. Frequent references in his mother's accounts to the payment of doctors and for drugs implies that she had to foot the bills for their attendance on her son. Then to Sir Robert's amusement, in addition to the doctors, messengers came almost hourly to make inquiries after Colin's health. They came from a young Dutch lady, Mademoiselle Mauritia de Nassau, who was then living with her elder sister, Lady Arlington, wife of the prime minister. These ladies (explains Lord Lindsay), with a third sister, Isabella, wife of the gallant Earl of Ossary, were daughters of Louis, Count of Beverwaert and Auverquerque (a natural son of Maurice, Prince of Orange) in Holland, by Elizabeth, Countess of Horn. The young Mauritia had been present at Colin's first presentation at court, 'and it seems', writes Colin's grandson, 'he was agreeable to her.'[3] Or, in other words, she fell passionately in love with him.

Colin, once recovered, was sent by Sir Robert to pay his respects to the young lady and, almost before he knew it, a day was fixed for their marriage. Plans for the wedding went swiftly ahead. Colin seems to have taken little part in the arrangements, the implications being that, although Mauritia genuinely loved him, he was pushed into the marriage by her ambitious and conniving sisters. Their social status was augmented when the Prince of Orange (later to be William III), himself now aged sixteen, sent a magnificent pair of emerald earrings as his gift. Perhaps, in doing so, he remembered the kindness of Balcarres' mother, his erstwhile governess, who had cared for him while her own son, now just about to be married, had been left behind in Scotland in the good Mr Forret's care.

All was arranged in what was, after all, a marriage of convenience, except that no one remembered to tell the young Earl of Balcarres, the bridegroom, of the time and date of the ceremony. The day of the marriage arrived, the wedding party was assembled and the bride waited in the church, but of the bridegroom there was not a sign. Someone sent running to Sir Robert Moray's house, burst in to find Colin Balcarres dressed in his nightgown and slippers, quietly eating his breakfast. Suddenly realising the enormity of what had happened, he leapt into his grandest doublet and hose, before bolting from the house in such a panic that he discovered, only on reaching the church, that the wedding-ring was still in his *escritoire*. One of the guests, realising his predicament as he searched frantically through his pockets, whispered that he would lend him a ring. He put his hand behind his back to receive it and, without looking at it, slipped it on the finger of his fair young bride. It was a mourning ring, engraved with the mort-head and crossed bones. Mauritia, when she saw it, swooned with shock as she recognised the emblems of mortality which she took to imply her doom. Recovering her senses she told all those present that she would die within the year. Sadly her presentiment was all too truly filled, for, less than twelve months afterwards, she died in childbirth.

All that remains of this sad interlude is a letter, written in French soon after her marriage, by Mauritia to Anna, the mother-in-law who had written to her, but whom she was fated never to know:

Madame,

Je ne scais en quells termes vous rendre très humbles graces de la bonté que vous avez en de m' écrire une letter si obligeante. Je vous assure, Madame, que j'en ai la reconnaissance que je dois, et que Milord Balcarres n'aurait pu épouser une personne qui tachera plus que je ferai à

cherchez les occasions de mériter votre amitié et à vous
témoigner en toute sorte de recontre avec combine de
respect et de soumission je suis,

Madame,

Votre très humble et obéissante fille et servante,

Maurisce de Balcarres.

Madam,

I know not in what terms to render you my very humble
thanks for your goodness in writing me so obliging a letter. I
assure you, Madam, that I am grateful of it as I ought to be,
and that my Lord Balcarres could not have espoused any one
who would endeavour more than I will do to seek out
occasion for meriting your friendship, and whereby to testify
to you in every matter of opportunity that amount of respect
and submission with which I am, Madam,

Your very humble and obedient daughter and servant,

Maurisce de Balcarres.[4]

Fortunately, if ironically, this poor little Dutch girl came with a
dowry of £16,000, with which her husband was able to pay off
part of the debt incurred by his father during the Civil War.

*

Countess Anna now decided to leave Balcarres. Remembering
how, on her own marriage, she had at first shared the castle
with her husband's mother and sister, she apparently thought it
only right that young married people should begin life in
absolute independence. Also, it seems unbeknown to almost
everyone, she now had plans of her own.

Before leaving, she carefully and methodically made inven-
tories of all important documents and family papers in her own
hand. This task completed, she then handed over an estate in

which the whole economical details of the establishment had been placed on a sound footing to her son. Believing that he would soon come to live there with his little Dutch bride, she wrote him a long letter setting forth most practical advice. Reminding him first of his heritage, she began:

My dear Son

We love our house, or land, or anything was our ancestors' more because it was theirs; so I expect that anything I can say to you will the more affect you because 'tis from your mother that loves you, wishes you well, and desires rather to see you a truly honest and virtuous man, fearing God, than possessor of all the riches the world can give. There are some that have power and riches; much to be pitied are such lovers of pleasures – they come to that, at last, they are troubled to hear anything that is not serious and which does not flatter them, though their actions merit reproof. But I am resolved neither to praise you, though I wish you deserve it from others, nor reprove what I think amiss in you; only will give you a motherly and hearty advice.

Having instructed him to love God above all else and to be loyal to the king, she warns him to beware of false friends: 'Nothing delights the heart of any man more than faithful and trusty friendship – to whom we may safely impart our mind . . . let not the least jealousy of your faithful friend enter into your mind, but whatever he do, think it was intended; in some cases it's better to be deceived than distrust.' Then, emphatically, she tells him to regard his wife 'as the dearest friend of your bosom' – to be chaste and constant to her, and to seek for his chief happiness at home.

Believe it, no man is happy but he that is so in his own house . . . When God blesseth you with children, as soon as they

can speak, by letting them know of God as much as they are
capable . . . look after them yourself and teach them their
devotions and morals. 'Tis like I may not see them at this
perfection, and you will be far abler to do this than I can
dictate to you, yet I let you see my good will and desire to
have you and yours happy for ever . . . My care hath been
great for you and your family, and may see by this I will be
always.[5]

 My dear son.
  Your kind Mother
  Anna Argyll.

This is the first indication that the widowed Anna, Countess of
Balcarres had married, a man himself a widower, Archibald
Campbell, 9th Earl of Argyll.

PART 2

CHAPTER 14

Lady Anna MacKenzie – Countess of Argyll

The second marriage, in 1670, of Lady Anna MacKenzie was no passionate love match as had been her first. Instead it was a sensible and practical arrangement between two middle-aged people in need of company and support. Archibald Argyll was a widower with seven small children, four boys and three girls, the eldest of whom, his heir Archibald, Lord Lorne, was only twelve. In Lady Anna he saw a woman of strong character who, devoted as she was to her own family, would surely care for his motherless brood.

Argyll, a small man, was known as 'the wee earl'. Portraits show him as sharp-featured, with hair reaching to his shoulders as was fashionable amongst the cavaliers. Renowned for his quick temper, he also had a passion for gadgets, having no fewer than twenty pockets sewn into one of his suits. Eccentric in some ways as Argyll appears to have been, for Lady Anna her marriage seemed to promise security, something she had lacked for many years. Also, as her son had a young wife, she felt it was only fair to let them have Balcarres Castle and the estate to themselves. For her part she now found herself the mistress of several houses, each of considerable size.

Firstly, in Argyll, there was Inveraray Castle, standing in a commanding position at the head of Loch Fyne, that great inlet of the sea, which penetrates into the mainland of the west coast, dividing Lorn and Mid-Argyll from Cowal. Secondly, in Cowal itself, there was the strong fortress of Carrick Castle near

Lochgoilhead on the north shore of Loch Long, while further south, on the Gareloch, Rosneath Castle was a favourite family resort. In addition to this there was the town house in Stirling, known as Argyll's Lodging, which stood around a courtyard and in view of the Castle Rock.[1]

Argyll bore his bride away in his own carriage with his coat of arms emblazoned on the door. Armed men rode before, behind and on either side of the carriage to protect against possible attack. For Countess Anna it was a poignant yet happy occasion. She would not have been human had she not felt at least some regret in leaving the familiar land of Fife, to which she had come as a girl of twelve some thirty-six years before. On the long journey they probably touched upon all that had happened over the years since they had first met in the wilds of Lochaber, during the Glencairn Rising of 1653. Argyll, who had then quarrelled so bitterly with Glencairn, had less than happy memories of how, when accused of treachery, he had ridden away with his men at dead of night. He probably also regretted the long-standing feud with his father, never entirely assuaged, over his adherence to the Royalist party which the marquess, who had reached an agreement with Cromwell, could neither understand nor forgive. In 1657 news must have reached Alexander and Anna Balcarres, while living in exile in Holland, of how Archibald, Lord Lorne, as he then was, had been cast into Edinburgh Castle as a prisoner for refusing to take an oath which, issued by the Protector's government, dictated that all the Royalists who had capitulated, must renounce their loyalty to the Stewarts and pledge allegiance to Cromwell's rule. It was there, in the castle courtyard, that Archibald, playing a game called 'bullets' with the English governor, was nearly killed as a bullet ricocheted with great force from a stone and hit him on the head. Unconscious for some hours, his life had been despaired of until a surgical operation known as trepanning (making an opening in the skull to relieve pressure on the brain) proved successful. Nonetheless there was some permanent damage, as a result of which he slept for some time every afternoon.

As they entered Argyll's own country they passed Kilchurn Castle, a tower-house surrounding a courtyard. This was the formidable fortress of Sir Colin Campbell of Glenorchy, the distant cousin chosen by his parents to be his foster father. Sir Colin and his lady, with no children of their own, had lavished care and affection upon the little boy, small even for his age, who had loved them greatly in return. In a childish hand and with doubtful spelling, he had once written, while on a visit to his parents, to 'my loving foster-father and respected friend the Lard of Glenvrquhey' begging him to send horses 'in all the heast and diligence' he could, to bring him and his tutor back from Inveraray.[2]

Then it was on past some of the most hard-fought territory of recent years. At Carness, on the east side of the River Aray, some of the burnt-out cottages still stood blackened by fire. Ironically, it had been the torching of the roofs, blazing to the night sky, which, seen from Inveraray, had given Argyll's father, the marquess, time to escape down Loch Fyne in a fishing boat. Behind him he had left the little town to be wrecked by ferocious enemies, but his castle, saved by its defences, had survived all attempts at assault.

Countess Anna must have sensed her husband's apprehension as they neared the old town, built round the mouth of the River Aray where it runs into Loch Fyne. This, as she knew, was the capital of his 'kingdom' of Argyll. Most likely uppermost in his mind was the dreadful day of 28 May, less then two years earlier, when, returning home from Dunoon, where he had gone on business, he had been met with the news that his wife had just died in childbirth, bearing their thirteenth child. Now, when he came with his new bride, he must have wondered how the seven surviving children of his first marriage would react to the intrusion of a stepmother.

He need not have worried. As Anna, handed out of the coach by her new husband, entered the old castle and climbed the spiral stair, she heard childish voices from above. Entering the nursery she found the seven little children, to whom she spoke in the Gaelic which she had learnt and still remembered from her own childhood in Ross-shire.

*

An account book of Archibald, 9th Earl of Argyll, for the year 1680, was the subject of a lecture read to the Society of Antiquaries of Scotland in January 1907. It throws an interesting light on the cost of running a large household at the end of the seventeenth century. No mention is made of meat, poultry and dairy products such as butter, which all came from the estate, where rents were paid partly in kind. However, fish was a large item. Herrings, bought at 7/ (Scots) per 100, were salted down in barrels in June, the beginning of the fishing season which lasted until December. Shellfish and oysters, for which Loch Fyne is now so famous, were bought, and a quarter-hundred of what is described as 'hard fish', presumably largely cod, haddock and whiting, cost £9.

Flour and biscuits, from a baker in Glasgow, came in by boat, as did the newly fashionable and expensive glasses, vinegar (wine) glasses, costing no less than 6/ each. The old pewter tankards and flagons, still good enough for everyday use, were mended by the local 'tinkler'. Soap came from Holland. Brandy and wine mostly from France. A hogshead of sack cost £162. Fuel was a large item, the bill for coal, also brought in by sea, amounting to £365, at 10/ a barrel. Peat, dragged down on sledges from the hills, cost 2/6 to 3/ a load. The cheapest candles were £2 18/ per stone, while those with cotton wicks were almost £1 dearer.

The children's clothes, boots and shoes were bought in

Edinburgh, as were golfballs, powder and lead for shooting, and arrows for archery. Fishing lines were bought in Greenock, probably to catch mackerel in Loch Fyne. There was by then a Grammar School in Inveraray, but the children, until old enough to go to the university, were taught at home. A Mr John Campbell, doctor of the grammar school in Glasgow, received an annual £40, while the fencing master, possibly from abroad, was paid £117, nearly three times as much, his large salary being justified by the vital need for young men to be proficient in self-defence.

The total sum for the year 1680 amounted to £18,417. It included 'sums expended by the Countess for charitable purposes',[3] this being a time when the old and sick amongst local people were entirely dependent on the charity of the Church and the landowners of the district.

*

It was now that Archibald, 9th Earl of Argyll, for the first time in his life, had the time and opportunity to enjoy his ancestral seat. The old castle, as shown by the topographer Thomas Sandby, stood not far from the present one surrounded by the small houses of the old town. The castle, dating from the late fifteenth century, typified the buildings of that period in that it was a hall-house four storeys high. Cellars on the ground floor were large enough to hold provisions for a garrison for several months. Above them was the great hall, where the earl dined with his retainers, who slept on the straw-covered floor before the fire at night. The bedrooms of the family and the solar, their private sitting room, occupied the third floor, while above them the garret gave extra sleeping room and storage space. From ramparts surrounding the rooftop sentries kept constant watch.

Outside the castle the earl enclosed gardens and laid out walks. He also developed a great interest in forestry, planting fruit trees, laburnums, plane trees, firs, oaks and in particular elms, for which he had a special love. On the advice of John Evelyn, one of the great horticulturists of the age, he took the greatest possible care in buying seeds and saplings and some of the beautiful old trees in the lime avenue may even date from this time.

There was also a vegetable garden in which, in the spring, the gardener planted out 700 bowkail (cabbages) and later gooseberry and currant bushes, at the cost of £21. Also he almost certainly planted onions, then much used in the Highlands, and possibly a few potatoes, which were at that time regarded as a luxury rather than as the main crop and sustenance of the local people as, in the next century, they became.

On a more commercial scale the earl developed the herring fishery, herring caught in Loch Fyne and salted in barrels being much in demand. Another business venture was the distillation of whisky, or uisge-beatha, as it then was called. The king and Lauderdale received presents of this fiery brew, in addition to which Argyll sent Lauderdale some honey from his own beehives so that he could make Atholl brose (a drink made with oatmeal, whisky and honey).

*

While the relationships between Countess Anna's newly extended family proved to be happy, her association with her cousin Lord Lauderdale now ended in a way that was extremely hurtful to her. Anna's last long letter to him went unanswered, and they do not seem to have spoken to each other or corresponded ever again. The reason for Lauderdale's coldness towards her was her marriage to Argyll.

When Lauderdale had come to Edinburgh as Lord High Commissioner, to preside over the Scottish parliament at the end of 1669, Argyll was one of the sumptuously dressed nobles who rode out to escort him into the city; then he had been shown special favour. It would seem that Lauderdale's mistrust developed later on, based on his fear of the enormous power which Argyll held in the north-west of Scotland. The strength of his influence in this area was such that Lauderdale saw him as a danger to the established government, believing that, in the event of renewed rebellion, he would rise in arms to suppress episcopacy by re-establishing Presbyterianism as the national religion in Scotland. It appears that Lauderdale's anger over his marriage to Lady Anna was augmented by the fear that Argyll would gain influence over her son, the young Lord Balcarres, whom Lauderdale regarded as his protégé and almost as his ward.

Lauderdale himself, if most historians are to be believed, had undergone a change of character. Gone was the young man with whom Alexander and Anna Balcarres, when they were first married, had spent such happy hours discussing the relative merits of authors in the library. The gangling young man of those days had grown gross at the court of Charles II. Presbyterian writers have accused him of becoming a libertine, given to over-indulgence as was King Charles himself. Lord Alexander Lindsay, however, having studied the Lauderdale letters, takes a kinder view, writing that:

> If the correspondence in question exhibits Charles and his Scottish advisers in a different light from that in which they are usually represented, all that can be said is that the evidence is that supplied by the men themselves, nor is it to be forgotten that writers, not of the popular school, have drawn Lauderdale's character, in particular, as that of a wise and conscientious statesman.[4]

Despite this it cannot be denied that Lauderdale is known to have fallen much under the influence of Lady Castlemaine, an avaricious and unscrupulous woman whose demands soon led him deeply into debt. Unattractive as he was – his portrait depicts him with a lugubrious expression and he is said to have covered everyone to whom he spoke directly with spittle, his tongue being too big for his mouth – he nonetheless held an attraction for women. Lady Dysart, sister of the 9th Earl of Argyll's first wife, set her cap at him to the point where his wife left him and went to live in France. There she died, whereupon, six weeks later, in 1671, Lauderdale married Lady Dysart.

Lauderdale's influence over Charles II remained paramount, however, rivalled only by that of Clarendon.

CHAPTER 15

Argyll's Lodging:
The House That Countess Anna Made Her Own

Countess Anna was then living largely in Argyll's Lodging in Stirling. This house, of all those belonging to her new husband, she felt to be her real home. First built in the sixteenth century, on the east side of the Castle Wynd, it overlooks the only road which links the castle to the town. Constructed on three sides of a courtyard the cobbles rang, in those days, with the stamping of hooves as carriages and other horse-drawn vehicles came and went. At that time, with its large gardens and open views across the Forth Valley to the Ochils, it resembled a country mansion rather than a town house.

Lord Lindsay, Anna's biographer, says that the house, then called the 'the Great Lodging' or Manor-place, had formerly belonged to Adam, Commendator (or lay owner) of Cambus-kenneth.[1] The Royal Commission of Ancient and Historical Monuments (RCAHMS), however, states that Argyll bought the house from Viscount Stirling in 1666, prior to his marriage with Countess Anna.[2] What actually happened was that Lord Stirling left the house to his son, from whom it was acquired by the Town Council, which proposed to use it as an almshouse. This scheme fell through and, taking Lord Lindsay's evidence to be correct, the house had been acquired from a previous owner by Argyll's father, the marquess. 'This edifice,' writes Lord Lindsay, 'with its garden, and another large house and various smaller tenements in the neighbourhood, together with a high loft and laigh seats within the Kirk of Stirling, just opposite to the pulpit, and an aisle or burial place belonging to the same property, had been conveyed to Argyll and the Countess, and the longest liver of them', in 1671, by an arrangement with the Marchioness of Argyll, widow of the marquess, who had then moved to Rosneath.[3]

In October 1674 Argyll settled the 'Lodging' and the above appendages more formally on the Countess Anna as her jointure house; and, on 1 June 1680, he made over to her the entire 'plenishings', furniture, and movables contained in it, seeing that: 'for the great love she bears us' she was content to accept the same in lieu of the more ample provision that she would have been entitled to if she survived him.[4] An inventory, signed by both, was made up on the occasion, and a brief analysis of it affords an interesting view of the domestic establishment of a great Scottish family in their town house at that time.

In the eight years since he had owned it Argyll had completed the south range and then added a south wing. The screen wall that bounds the west side of the courtyard was another addition of his time. Today, only a small part of the wing, which was largely destroyed in the nineteenth century, remains, but a pediment above the tower doorway, surmounted by a stone carving of a vase of flowers, clearly displays, in raised figures, the date of 1674. From the doorway, a turnpike stair leads to the first floor where, in the Great, or Laigh Hall, a carving of an earl's coronet is surmounted by a boar's head, crest of the now ducal family of Argyll. Here also, a small boudoir, attached to the main reception room, was built and furnished especially for Countess Anna. The hangings and some of the furniture were of her own choice, thus making the house, which had few if any connections with Argyll's first wife, very much her own.

Lord Lindsay describes the house and its contents in full:

> The principal apartments consisted of the 'Laigh Hall', pro-
> vided with twelve folding tables and thirty chairs; the drawing-
> room, or 'Laigh drawing-room', furnished with two very great

looking-glasses and a chair of state, with purple curtains, or canopy; 'My Lord and Lady's chamber', 'my Lady's closet' [what we would now call her boudoir, or sitting room], the apartments of Lady Jean Campbell, Argyll's daughter, [those of Anna's youngest daughter, Sophia, Henrietta being then married] and of Lord Lorne, Argyll's eldest son, formed three suites. Each consisted of an outer chamber or lobby, a central room, and an inner or smaller closet, Lady Jean's opening on to the garden. The 'grey-room' with its closet, the 'wardrobe', apparently a very important room, furnished with massive fir chests containing stores of cloth, hangings, etc, for the most part not made up, with the 'Tailzior's' or tailor's room adjacent, where the materials were shaped and put together when needed. There were various offices, the 'Master of the Household's room', the 'glass-room', devoted to crockery, trenchers etc, the 'great kitchen', provided with two grates, and the 'little kitchen' with a small grate, and all the necessary materials for cookery. There were also a Pantry, an Ale cellar, the Laigh dining-room, or servant's hall and the 'Woman-house' [apparently a separate two-storey wing provided with 'stent trees' for linen, 'owl' or 'wool-wheels' for spinning wool, 'lint-wheels' for flax and 'gairne-roundills' or boards for making oat-cakes] besides the bake-house and the brew-house, the invariable appendages of old Scottish mansions.

Among the 'plenishing' every early stage of invention was represented, from the rood form and humble joint stool, the first creations of civilisations, to the 'black wooden chair' with its seat super-induced with richly wrought tapestry and 'needle-work sublime', fraught to our recollection with

> The peony spread wide,
> The full-blown rose, the shepherd and his lass,
> Lap-dog and lambkin with black staring eyes,
> And parrots with twin cherries in their beak.

On the walls hung 'my Lord's picture, in a little gilded frame', and 'Mr Baxter's picture', while 'fifteen painted fancies' further decorated the apartment. The hangings were of stamped purple, and the tablecloth to match. Such was the Countess Anna's sanctum, her household goods, some of them probably dear to her from old Balcarres associations, in her new home.[5]

*

With their mother, in the early winter of 1674, were Lady Henrietta and Lady Sophia Lindsay the two younger daughters of her first marriage to Lord Balcarres. Both young women, now in their early twenties, were firm supporters of the Covenanting party, as indeed were their mother and step-father. The two were vastly different in character. Lady Henrietta, quiet and withdrawn, was very pious, as is proved by the diary in which she meticulously recorded her thoughts. She writes of 'the cheerful piety' of her mother's servants, as well as of her mother's early instruction. The love of religions sprang up in her heart in childhood and, at sixteen years of age, induced her solemnly to dedicate herself, after her best endeavour, to the 'service of her Redeemer'.[6]

This must have occurred during the brief period when, following her mother's second marriage, she lived with her brother, Earl Colin, at Balcarres, for she describes how, for many weeks after thus pledging herself to God, her greatest joy was to sing the forty-fifth psalm while walking in the quiet and sheltered woods round the castle.

At that time Henrietta appears to have been obsessed to the point of fanaticism with her newly discovered faith. She began to have visions and dreams and she lived in constant terror of Satan appearing in bodily shape. One day, when praying secretly, she saw him, in the form of a black lion roaring in

fury, but in the same instant, he was caught and held im-
movable within the coils of a chain. Convinced then that he
could no longer hurt her, she lost her slavish fear.

Despite her release from this particular phobia, Henrietta's
nervous disposition, and obviously unbalanced state of mind,
may have been one reason, probably the main one, why she
and her younger sister Sophia were, on their mother's insistence, removed from the care of their brother at Balcarres, and
taken to live with her and their stepfather, the Earl of Argyll.

Lady Sophia, who much resembled her mother and was
already renowned for her beauty and vivacity, was also well
known for her strong character. Outspoken in her convictions,
she paid small heed to authority of any kind. She had for some
time been a friend of a Mr Blackadder, a well-known preacher,
to the point where she had attended his conventicles from time
to time. Most notably, she must have been amongst the crowd
which gathered in 1674 on the Craig of Balcarres, then bare of
trees, to hear him preach with such passion that many of those
gathered were sobbing aloud with emotion.

Blackadder's son was an apprentice in a shop in Stirling and,
in November 1674, he was arrested and sent to prison with
several others for attending illegal religious meetings, as pro-
scribed by the Parliament of 1673. Stirling's Old Town Jail,
which backs onto the town walls, was renowned as being the
worst in Scotland. Prisoners had to survive largely on poorly
cooked thin gruel. Forced to sleep on the floor on vermin-
infested straw, their condition was made more wretched in the
shortening days of November as the weather became increasingly cold. Many caught typhoid – the dreaded jail fever spread
by lice – and even those not infected suffered from pain in their
joints as damp oozed from stone walls. Furiously resentful at his
incarceration, young Blackadder attributed all his misfortune
to the violence and ignorance of the Provost of Stirling.

Lying in prison, in fear of his life, he was, to his enormous surprise and delight, visited by both Countess Anna's daughters and her stepdaughter, Lady Jean Campbell. The three ladies caused great excitement to the inmates of the jail as they swept into its drab and foul-smelling interior with a great rustling of the silks, satins and taffeta of their gowns. All three were horrified by what they found. The ladies gasped, holding handkerchiefs to their noses but Sophia, irrepressible as usual, leapt up on a bench and arraigned the hapless Provost of Stirling in no uncertain terms, telling him, to his face, that it was he who deserved to be hanged for his unjust imprisonment of the young men.

The provost, greatly affronted, complained to the Privy Council for which 'the good Earl was like to be brought to much trouble about it'.[7] Fortunately, however, young Blackadder's brother, who, in addition to being a doctor, had some knowledge of the law, managed to prove that he had been condemned to prison on illegal grounds and he was subsequently released.

CHAPTER 16

Argyll's Acquisition of the Isle of Mull, and the Gathering of the Highland Host

Argyll must have been relieved to be spared further litigation, being deeply involved in a law suit of his own concerning possession of the Isle of Mull. The island, held by the Mac-Leans of Duart since the fourteenth century, had been pledged by Sir Allan MacLean to the Marquess of Argyll in return for a loan of 500,000 merks, over £27,000 sterling, a debt incurred in the service of Charles I during the Civil War. Argyll now claimed repayment of the money owed to his father. The case came before the Court of Session, which ruled in his favour, ordering that payment must be made and the land sold if necessary, to meet the cost. Payment was not made, however, and over the next two years Argyll was forced to use both military and legal means to win the island, and at one point had large numbers of men defending the coast of Lorn.

Argyll, being Lauderdale's greatest supporter in Scotland at this time, had his powerful backing. Lauderdale, for his part, relied greatly upon Argyll's aid against his own enemies who, headed by the Duke of Hamilton, were clamouring for his removal from the office of Royal Commissioner in Scotland. Eventually, in June 1676, the dispute came before three members of the Scottish Privy Council who, after debating for over a year, decreed in favour of Argyll. Despite this, however, Argyll, with the aid of 300 regular troops, was forced to take the island by storm. On 1 November 1679 King Charles, in a letter, declared himself satisfied with all that had been done. The settlement was completed and the island of Mull then became part of the already enormous landholding of the Campbells in the north-west Highlands and the Isles.

*

By the late 1670s the influence of the Presbyterians in Scotland was once again causing anxiety among those in power. Episcopacy had been restored by King Charles II on his return to the throne, and various Acts had since been passed restricting the activities of the Nonconformists. One, known as the 'Bishops' dragnet', decreed that anyone who did not attend their local church was liable to a heavy fine. It was so greatly resented that ministers, many of them ousted from their parishes, held secret conventicles in the woods and fields, well hidden from public view.

Despite the fact that Argyll, a known Covenanter, had come under serious suspicion of treachery and in 1663 only narrowly escaped execution, his homeland of Inveraray had become a haven in the religious vortex that was sweeping most of Scotland during the 1660s. When, on 7 June 1669, a letter reached Edinburgh from Charles II offering indulgence to the Presbyterian ministers who had been turned out of their livings seven years before, six of these were installed in churches in Argyllshire of which Argyll himself was the patron.

However, by 1677 Lauderdale, alarmed by reports of armed men taking part in conventicles in the south-west of Scotland, introduced a bond by which all landlords in the disaffected areas were to be forced, together with their adherents (who included their tenants and all who lived on their estates), to forego all conventicles, and to arrest all 'vagrant preachers' and others of suspicious character and deliver them to the authorities.

In addition to this, Lauderdale conceived the idea of maintaining order in rebellious areas with men enlisted from the Highlands. At the end of the year letters were sent by the Privy Council to the great landowners in the north of Scotland, including the Marquess of Atholl and the Earl of Moray, asking them to raise men to form an army of occupation. This was not difficult. The Highlanders were all too keen for a chance to plunder the Lowlands, but it is notable that the Earl of Argyll, still embroiled in his struggle to win Mull, claimed that his fencible men could not be spared from defending the coast of Lorn and refused to participate in this scheme. Despite the validity of his excuse, his refusal to take action against the more extreme party of the Covenanters was regarded with grave suspicion as neither Archibald Argyll himself nor his Countess Anna made any secret of their devout Presbyterianism.

*

On 14 January 1678, the Highland host convened upon Stirling. Most were caterans, in the words of the historian, Woodrow, 'the very scum of that uncivilised country'.[1] His words proved only too true. At sight of the well-furnished houses in Stirling the plundering began. In Argyll's Lodging Countess Anna, having ordered her servants to lock and bar the doors and windows, saw the smoke of burning roofs rising above the town.

Fortunately, the Highland freebooters soon marched off to Glasgow to cause further havoc both in the city itself and along the way. From there, where they were joined by a large detachment of regular soldiers and militia, they advanced into the counties of Lanark, Renfrew and Ayrshire where, under the orders of the Privy Council, they seized arms, horses and anything of value as well as trying to force the inhabitants to take the bond. In the last instance they were singularly unsuccessful. The stout-hearted people of the Lowland shires resisted them to the point where Lauderdale, when told of it, 'behaved like a madman, bearing his arms above the elbows and swearing by the ineffable name of God that he would force the recusants to give way'.[2]

Subsequently, in view of their failure to accomplish the main object of their mission, the Highland troops were withdrawn. Once again the doors and shutters of Argyll's Lodging were barred as they returned through Stirling. The men, long-haired and bearded, wrapped in plaids matted with mud from sleeping on the ground, staggered under household articles such as cooking pots and clothing that they had looted from Lowland homes, while their officers, reputedly, walked equally unsteadily, weighed down by pockets filled with gold.

CHAPTER 17

Conspiracy, Murder and Rebellion

In the following year, 1678, Lauderdale's position in England was greatly threatened by the revelations of Titus Oates. This Anglican churchman who, having converted to Catholicism and become a Jesuit, had then abandoned that faith, had declared that Sir George Wakeman, the king's physician, and Edward Coleman, secretary to the Duchess of York, were planning to kill King Charles by poison. He swore that their ultimate aim, once they had prevented the accession of Charles's brother James, the Duke of York, was the conquest of England for France. Oates' claim, fantastic as it would appear, was substantiated by the discovery of highly suspicious correspondence between Coleman and the confessor of Louis XIV.[1]

From this it was taken that Charles II had plotted with the French king for the overthrow of English freedom and religion. The Duke of York, a Catholic, had to flee to the Continent, the Cavalier Parliament, which had been in power since the Restoration, was dissolved, and the Earl of Shaftesbury, leader of the Whigs, seized the chance to attack Lauderdale's Scottish regime.

Lauderdale survived, thanks to the continued favour of King Charles, but his influence was undermined when Shaftesbury, in a rousing speech to the House of Lords, denounced the persecution of the Presbyterians in Scotland. 'Popery was intended to precede slavery in England, and slavery had been the forerunner of Popery in Scotland'[2] he declared. The words were hardly out of his mouth before forty copies of his speech were being carried to Edinburgh in a post chaise. Distributed amongst Lauderdale's enemies, they actively encouraged rebellion.

Trouble first broke out at Lesmahagow, in Clydesdale, on Sunday, 30 March 1679. When the commander of the army, which was stationed at Lanark, was told that a conventicle was to be held there, he sent a detachment of soldiers under a Lieutenant Dalziel with instructions to break up the meeting and arrest the ringleaders. This unfortunate young man, who expected little or no resistance, was confronted by a well-armed force, about 360-strong, which immediately attacked. He himself was mortally wounded and carried as a prisoner from the field.

A month later an armed party of Covenanters was told that the coach in which the Scottish episcopal primate, Archbishop Sharp, was travelling to St Andrews was approaching. Overtaking his carriage on Magus Moor, they dragged him out of it and, despite the screams and pleas for mercy from both himself and the daughter who was with him, hacked him to death with their swords. Shortly after this, James Graham of Claverhouse, later to be better known as 'Bonnie Dundee, a young man of thirty-three', who had served first in the French army and then with the Dutch under William of Orange, was given command of a newly raised troop of horse, which was later to become the famous regiment of the Scots Greys. With them he attacked a group of Covenanters, who were holding a conventicle on boggy ground near the farm of Drumclog, in Lanarkshire, some sixteen miles from Glasgow. Although armed largely with fusils and pitchforks, they roundly defeated him. He rode away with the voice of a Covenanter asking him if he wanted to stay for the afternoon service ringing in his ears.[3]

Writing to the Earl of Linlithgow, Commander-in-Chief, Claverhouse gave him a grave warning. 'What these rogues will do next I know not, but the country was floking to them from all hands. This may be counted the beginning of the rebellion.'[4]

The Privy Council, thoroughly alarmed, having already called out the militia in the east and south of Scotland, had ordered the earls of Argyll and Caithness to rise in arms to suppress the rebels. Argyll, still occupied in taking possession of Mull from the MacLeans, was given peremptory orders 'to disentangle himself as soon as possible from his present engagements, and to repair to the camp of the Earl of Linlithgow with all the men he could raise':

> We doubt not of your Lordship's readiness, upon all occasions to give commendable proofs of your loyalty and duty to his sacred majesty, and you cannot give a more signal testimony thereof, and of your zeal for the peace and happiness of this kingdom, than by a seasonable assistance against these rebels, and so we cannot but expect a cheerful and ready compliance from your lordship with so just and necessary desire.[5]

So ran the summons, which has been taken by some historians to imply that Argyll was under strong suspicion of being secretly sympathetic to the Covenanters. This seems further indicated by the fact that several members of the Privy Council urged the revocation of the commission granted to him just before the Battle of Drumclog, to maintain peace in the Highlands and the Isles. This, combined with the fact that marked indulgence was shown to many of his enemies, indicates that, as a known supporter of Lauderdale, now in conflict with the party in England headed by Shaftesbury, he stood in a position of great danger.

In England Shaftesbury pressed for Lauderdale to resign as Secretary of State for Scotland. Charles II, however, stood by his long-term minister. A compromise was reached when the command of the Duke of Monmouth (the Protestant son of the king and Lucy Walters), who was already Commander-in-Chief of the army in England, was extended to Scotland. Monmouth, a young man of thirty, energetic if not a great strategist, and possessed of both his father's looks and his charm, acted with great expediency. In a very short time he had mustered an army of three regiments of foot soldiers, three of cavalry, eight hundred dragoons and three troops of grenadiers. In addition he assembled enough cannon and ammunition to effect a long siege. Leaving London on 15 June 1679, he took only three days to reach Edinburgh where, on arrival, he was immediately made a member of the Privy Council.

The Army of the Covenant, largely untrained, was totally defeated by the Royal army at Bothwell Bridge, which spans the Clyde at Hamilton. Monmouth, who had orders to be as lenient as possible, stopped his men from killing their prisoners. Despite his clemency however, 200 of them were to die in a shipwreck off the coast of Orkney while being sent to the plantations in America.[6]

Monmouth's popularity in Scotland, where he had won many hearts by his leniency to the prisoners at Bothwell Bridge, steadily increased. He was also well liked in England, particularly by the Protestant factor of the community, who dreaded the probable ascension of a Roman Catholic king. A climax was reached when Charles II lay dangerously ill with a fever that was probably malaria. Then the likelihood of his brother succeeding him brought renewed threat of civil war.

Fortunately the king recovered, saved by the 'Jesuit's powder', an early form of quinine extracted from the bark of the *cinchona* in South America.[7] However, the Duke of York had in the meantime returned from Brussels in disguise. Monmouth, who in the event of the death of his father was York's great rival for the throne, did his best to prevent this, but Charles II preferred the interests of his brother, as being descended in the right line, over those of his son. Therefore, despite his popularity, it was Monmouth, stripped of his commands, who was told to retire to Holland and Shaftesbury, his chief supporter and deadly rival of Lauderdale, was dismissed from the Privy Council, while the Duke of York was told, supposedly, to leave England.

*

Meanwhile, in Scotland, the families of Lauderdale and Argyll, already related through Countess Anna, were further united by the marriage of Argyll's son and heir, Lord Lorne, to Lauderdale's stepdaughter, Lady Elizabeth Tollemache: Elizabeth was the daughter of the Countess of Dysart by her first marriage to Sir Lionel Tollemache. This redoubtable lady (countess in her own right) had become Lauderdale's second wife. Ties between the two families were then further increased when Lady Anne Campbell, Argyll's second daughter, married Lauderdale's nephew, who eventually succeeded to his title. Lauderdale himself, now very old and infirm, resigned as Secretary of State for Scotland in 1680, to be replaced by the Earl of Moray.

Another family wedding of the year 1678 was that of the pious Lady Henrietta Lindsay, the second of Countess Anna's daughters, to Sir Duncan Campbell of Auchinbreck. The family of Auchinbreck, descended from Duncan Campbell of Kilmichael, a younger son of Sir Duncan Campbell of Lochawe, 1st Lord Campbell, who lived in the latter part of the fourteenth century, was then powerful in Argyll. Their land stretched from the west coast of Loch Fyne to the area around Kilmartin, where the 'Bishop's Castle' of Carnasserie was one of their strongholds.[8] Two years later, in 1680, Lady Henrietta and her little son, then just a year old, made a visit to her mother in the old castle of Inveraray. Countess Anna spent

147

happy hours looking after young Jamie. A devoted mother, she made much of her one and only grandson who, in his own old age, was to become a fervent adherent of Prince Charles Edward in the Rising of 1745.

Shortly after this there was a family reunion in Kintyre. Records do not state where this took place. The old castle of Kilkerran, to the south-east of Campbeltown, is said to have been uninhabitable by the second decade of the seventeenth century.[9] For this reason the Royal Castle of Tarbert, of which Argyll was the captain (an honour which remains with the family to this day) would seem to have been the most likely rendezvous. The castle, in its impregnable position overlooking the entrance to Tarbert harbour, was certainly a suitable location for a large gathering. Built to withstand a long siege, the hall house towered above a huge cellar where grain and salted-down carcasses could be stored for months on end. The three main floors, surmounted by a garret, could accommodate the family itself. In addition, the four ranges of buildings around the courtyard of the inner bailey, designed to hold the garrison, could be used to provide extra sleeping space.[10]

All that we know for certain is that the gathering in some respects resembled the biblical miracle of the loaves and fishes which fed the assembled multitude on the shores of the Lake of Galilee. Lady Henrietta, still fanatically religious, wrote that: 'Most of the late Earl's family and my mother's, being a numerous company, had a cheerful meeting in Cantyre, the sacrament being administered there two days following together. And indeed, as this meal was doubled to many, so there wanted not a long journey to many to go in the strength of it.'[11]

This proved to be the last happy interlude before the family of Argyll was once more embroiled in conflict.[12]

*

The Duke of York was sent by his brother Charles II to replace Lauderdale as Royal Commissioner in Scotland. Reaching Edinburgh in November 1679, he was at once installed in the Royal Palace of Holyrood.

In February 1681 the duke was entertained by the Earl and Countess of Argyll at Argyll's Lodging in Stirling. His second wife, the lovely Mary of Modena, is not mentioned in accounts of the visit, which suggests that he came without her. The excitement at Argyll's Lodging is easy to imagine. The damask tablecloths and napkins, and Countess Anna's precious pots, which had been sent over to Scotland from Holland, were unearthed. The kitchen staff were set to preparing roasts of meat and to stuffing and cooking a variety of game birds. Puddings were concocted and wine heated. Silver and brass candlesticks were polished and candles blazed in the sconces on the walls.

The duke was entertained as befits a royal personage. He showed great deference to his hostess, Countess Anna, who, although now aged sixty, still had the bearing and fine features, especially those beautiful brown eyes, of a woman of much younger years. She, for her part, must have felt pleased, and perhaps relieved, that an evening of such importance had seemed to be such an outstanding success.

Before the dinner she had feared discord, being well aware of the short tempers of both her husband and their guest. Little could she guess, as the two withdrew from the dining room to another chamber for private conversation, the duke towering above the earl, how this most memorable of evenings was yet to end . . .

The Duke was pleased to thank the Earl for his hospitality and kindness, and to ask the Earl wherein he was able to show the sense he had of the favour he had done him. The Earl humbly thanked his Highness for his goodness and said his favour would more than recompense. The Duke said 'My Lord, if you will do one thing you may be the greatest man in Scotland.' The Earl begged to know what that was. The Duke said it was a thing in doing which he would singularly oblige him. The Earl again humbly desired to know what that was. The Duke replied that all he desired of him was that he would change the worst of religions for the best.

Argyll, infuriated, 'gave him a very cutting answer, and [it was noticed] that henceforth the Duke's coldness of manner towards him marked the depth of his resentment which the rejection of his proposal had occasioned'.[13]

The die was cast. Argyll's enemies, knowing all too soon how he had displeased the Duke of York, now saw their chance to ruin him.

PART 3

CHAPTER 18

The Test Act

And the enemies gathered like birds of prey . . .

The Scottish Parliament met in Edinburgh on 28 July 1681. As was customary, the ceremony of 'riding' from Holyrood House to the place of the assembly was performed with great splendour. Argyll carried the crown up the street now known as 'the Royal Mile'. On either side, cheering people on the roadsides jostled and elbowed each other out of the way to get a better view. Above them, in the tall houses of the old town, handkerchiefs waved from windows crammed with spectators greeting the procession with cries of joy and acclamation. It was a splendid sight. Little could Argyll, or anyone connected with him, have guessed at the significance of that walk which, only four years later, he would make again under circumstances then fortunately unforeseen.

The two main reasons for this parliament were, firstly, to enact the further repression of the more extreme Covenanters and, secondly and most importantly, to secure the succession of the Roman Catholic Duke of York to the throne. The first Act passed by the Assembly ratified the laws which already existed to protect the Protestant religion. Those which condemned the Roman Catholic faith were, on the decision of the Committee of Articles, omitted to avoid offending the Duke of York. Argyll, however, oblivious to the risks involved, proposed that a clause to enforce these laws should be contained within the decree. In this suggestion he was supported by the advocate,

Sir George Lockhart, and by Sir James Dalrymple, President of the Court of Session. Subsequently, without a vote being taken, the clause was included in the Act.

The duke, although thus insulted, warned Argyll that his foes were waiting to attack. The Earl of Errol, in particular, backed by other men of influence, was about to claim recompense from the Argyll estates for debts incurred by the Marquess (Argyll's father) during both the Civil War and the subsequent period of Commonwealth rule. The matter was investigated and Argyll was able to prove that he had inherited only part of his father's property and that in the list of those to whom money was owed, Errol's name was not included.

Thus, on that account, he was cleared. But his enemies, knowing that he was now out of favour with the Duke of York, continued their persecution. Next came the declaration from the Lord Advocate, Sir George Mackenzie, known due to the barbarity of his judgments as 'Bloody Mackenzie'. He announced that he had been ordered to strip Argyll of his hereditary offices of Sheriff and Justiciar General of Argyllshire and the Isles. Here again, however, Argyll was triumphant, being able to prove that these offices, granted to his ancestors in the fifteenth century, had been expressly renewed to himself by Charles II only nine years before, in 1672.

It was now over 200 years since Duncan, Lord Campbell of Lochow, had been appointed the king's Justiciary and Lord Lieutenant of the county of Argyll in 1445, by King James II of Scotland. The rights of regality, then conferred upon him, had given him the authority of dictating life or death – the power of pit and gallows – of those within the sphere of his superiority. Only the crime of high treason could be referred to the Circuit Courts, which, presided over by the king, were held at specified intervals in the main cities of the kingdom. In 1528 the family's predominance had increased when Colin, 3rd Earl of Argyll, had been confirmed not only as Sheriff of Argyll, but as Justice

General of Scotland and Master of the Royal Household. These offices, held previously by his predecessors as individuals, had, at that time, been confirmed as hereditary.[1]

This situation had lasted for a full hundred years until 3 April 1628, when Lord Lorne (later to become the Marquess of Argyll) had resigned the hereditary office of Justice General of all Scotland to King Charles I. In return the king had confirmed that the office of Justiciar of Argyll and the Western Isles and wherever else Argyll had land in Scotland, should remain with his family in perpetuity.

Next came a claim that Archibald, Earl of Argyll's father's estates, when forfeited after his execution, had been annexed to the Crown. This also was proved false. The estates which the king had restored to Argyll had been entirely at his own disposal. Argyll, seeing the ridiculous side of it, remarked with some bitterness that annexing the property to the Crown was the last thing those who had been active against his father would have desired, 'as the secret of their activity had been the expectation of dividing the spoil amongst themselves'.[2]

The Duke of York protected his own interests in this parliament of July 1681 by an Act which proclaimed that no difference of religions and no law passed by any assembly could prevent the nearest heir to the throne from becoming king. His right to succeed his brother was then further ensured by the statute known as the Test Act by which all those who would not be subservient to the monarch were excluded from holding office in either Church or State. From then on anyone in any form of official capacity had to swear that they 'sincerely professed the true Protestant religion', contained in the Confessions of Faith of the first parliament of James VI in 1567. More importantly, they had also to swear that the king's majesty was the only supreme governor of the realm, that it was unlawful for people to join covenants or leagues without the king's permission, that they were under no obligation from either the National Covenant or the Solemn League and Covenant and that they would never refuse the king's ruling in matters of religion and State.

This last clause, amounting to a direct denial of the affirmation contained in the Confession of Faith that 'Jesus Christ was the only head of the church' was plainly perjurious. The Act implied, moreover, that the king could now impose any form of religion he chose upon his subjects. Moreover, it was proposed that members of the royal family could still hold office without subscribing to the Act.

Argyll stated openly that it was essential to the wellbeing of the nation 'that King and people were of one religion and that they were so by law'.[3] Despite his strong objections, however, the Test Act was carried through and orders went out that all holding office in either a lay or ecclesiastical capacity must take the oath before 1 January 1682.

Parliament was then adjourned but hardly had that happened before Argyll's enemies were again demanding that he be stripped of his heritable offices and forced to pay the debts which they claimed his father had incurred. Argyll, in an interview with the Duke of York, said that he would be willing to submit the matter to the king, and if, after he had been heard in defence of his rights, His Majesty were to request the surrender of these offices, he would be willing to do so.[4]

The duke then sensibly suggested that Argyll should produce the royal warrants and charters which confirmed his rights to the hereditary offices which were now so hotly in dispute. The earl, thus instructed, left Edinburgh to travel across Scotland to Inveraray where, from the charter-room of the old castle, he took the documents that were so essential to his claims.

*

Archibald Argyll had hardly left the capital before he was writing to the Earl of Moray, successor to Lauderdale as

Secretary of State, to ask for an interview with the king. This was at first sanctioned, but then he was told that the king would see him only on condition that he subscribe to the Test Act.

Reaching Glasgow on his way back to Edinburgh, Argyll received further proof of the disfavour in which he now stood. The Duke of York was greatly offended because he had written to the Earl of Moray instead of to himself. It would seem that it was partly for this reason that he had been dismissed from the Court of Session of which he had been an Extraordinary Lord since 1674.

Believing then that he had two full months before he could be compelled to take the Test Act, he was both surprised and angered to be summoned to a special meeting of the Privy Council arranged, so he was told, for the express reason of forcing him to take the Test Act. He at once asked to see the Duke of York and was granted an interview with him, in his bedroom after supper, at Holyrood. Argyll told him that he now had the writs and charters which proved, without doubt, his rights to his hereditary offices. Then he demanded to know if it were true that he had been dismissed from the Court of Session. The duke replied in the affirmative and, when asked what would happen next, he said he simply did not know.

This was too much for Argyll to take without protest. He told the duke bluntly that he had never curried favour from the king and that he had served him faithfully for over thirty years. 'I know I have enemies, but they shall never make me alter my dutie and resolution to serve His Majesty. I have served His Majesty in armes, and in his judicatures, when I knew I had enemies on my right and on my left, and I will doe so still. But if any have power to render His Majesty or Your Highness jealous of me, it will make my service the more useful to both and the less comfortable to myself.'[5]

The duke's only reply was that he knew no more about the matter than what he had already told him. It was now very late

and Argyll suggested that he should wait on him to show him
his documents, at some other time. Then, before leaving, he
asked if it was true that he had been ordered to appear before
his fellow members of the Privy Council to swear allegiance to
the Test Act the next day. The duke replied that this was so but
that he could, if he liked, postpone the summons until Thursday, 3 November, when the next ordinary meeting of the
Council would assemble.

Argyll, thus given time for consideration, prepared a written
explanation of the terms under which he would take the Test
Act. The Bishop of Edinburgh told him that this would be very
kindly received. Thus, before kneeling down to commit himself
to the Test Act he read his prepared declaration:

> I have considered the Test, and am very desirous to give
> obedience as far as I can. I am confident the Parliament
> never intended to impose contradictory oaths. Therefore I
> think no man can explain it but for himself. Accordingly, I
> take it, as far as it is consistent with itself and the Protestant
> religion. And I do declare that I mean not to bind up myself
> in my station, and in a lawful way to wish and endeavour any
> alteration I think to the advantage of Church or State, not
> repugnant to the Protestant Religion and my Loyalty. And
> this I understand as a part of my oath.[6]

The commitment once made, Argyll sat beside the duke, who
spoke to him in the most friendly terms. The next day,
however, he was received with open hostility, a clear indication
that York had been influenced by the insinuations of his
enemies that his words of explanation concerning the oath
had amounted to treason. The situation within the Council
Chamber became more tense when, as Commissioner of the
Treasury, Argyll had to take the oath again and, on the
insistence of the Earl of Roxburgh, to repeat his words of

explanation. Taking the paper on which the words were written, from one of his many pockets, he read them out loud. He was then told to go into an adjoining room and made to wait while the members of the Council debated on what they had just heard. Called back, he was commanded to sign the paper, which was then taken out of his hands.

His enemies, exultant, realised that they now had the evidence they needed to prove him a dissenter to the government. The duke himself, making no effort to hide his now open dislike, told him that he 'had designed to bring trouble upon an handful of poor Catholicks, that would live peaceably however they were used, but it should light upon others'.[7] Then, in a final injunction, he told Argyll that he must not leave Edinburgh till he saw him again.

Subsequently, on Tuesday, 8 November 1681, when the council met again, a clerk was dispatched with an order to Argyll to surrender himself to the Deputy-Governor of Edinburgh Castle by twelve o'clock on the following day.

Argyll obeyed. It is said that 'some of his relations and persons of quality'[8] wanted to go with him but that this he firmly refused. It seems logical to believe that Countess Anna was amongst the little group who saw him go, alone in a hackney coach, to the great fortress on the rock. There on that bleak winter's day, as a bitter wind blew from the North Sea through Edinburgh's narrow streets, she must have felt once again, as when her beloved first husband had died, that her world was falling apart. Nonetheless, from all that we know of her, it is certain that even now, under the most difficult and tragic of circumstances, she would have remained stoical, erect and dignified in her bearing, refusing to let her feelings betray her with as much as a single tear.

CHAPTER 19

The Death Sentence Confirmed

Courageous as she is known to have been, the days following her husband's imprisonment in Edinburgh Castle must, for Countess Anna, have had the semblance of a nightmare. While Argyll was held in Edinburgh Castle she did not know when he would be tried and, most probably, executed on a capital charge.

The trial began on Monday, 12 December 1681. Argyll, accompanied by the Governor of Edinburgh Castle, was taken in a coach to the Court of Justiciary. The indictment accusing him of treason having been read out, he then made an impassioned speech in his defence, pointing out how he had steadfastly supported the royal cause at the time of the Commonwealth and ending with the words 'God save the king'.[1] In confirmation he produced four letters, one written by Charles II in Cologne, two from General Middleton and one from the Earl of Glencairn, all of which testified to his unswerving loyalty to the Crown.

The arguments, both for the defence and the prosecution, were continued by the advocates employed to act on the case. Argyll was defended by Sir George Lockhart, the famous lawyer who had already supported him over the inclusion of the clause prohibiting 'Popery' in the Test Act. Lockhart spoke for three hours. He pointed out to the assembled court that 'many others had accused the Act of contradictions and inconsistencies and that it had not been suggested that they had been guilty of criminal conduct and should be prosecuted for it.'[2]

In reply to this the Lord Advocate, Sir George Mackenzie, appearing for the prosecution, declared that 'this excellent Test' had been drawn up to secure both the Protestant religion and the Crown, the parliament 'did positively ordain that this Oath should be taken in the plain genuine meaning of the words, without any evasion whatsoever'. He claimed that Argyll, by stipulating that he agreed to the Test Act 'as far as it is consistent with itself and the Protestant religion', had evaded the main issue and in doing so had committed perjury.[3]

The public hearing of the case ended at nine o'clock on the evening of 12 December. The judges, however, continued to prepare their interlocutor until two o'clock in the morning. Only four of the lords, together with the Justice General, had been present throughout the proceedings. The fifth judge, Lord Nairn, who was very old and suffering from partial dementia, had gone home almost as the trial began. Now, however, as two of the judges decreed that Argyll had made a libellous statement, and two that he had not, it was necessary to summon Lord Nairn to give a casting vote.

Woken up and hustled into his clothes, the aged gentleman, on reaching the court, had the indictment read to him by a clerk before dozing off again. Then, prodded into conscious-ness, he gave his vote in favour of Argyll being found guilty of the crimes with which he was charged. Thus, in what amounted to a farce worthy of the theatre, the little earl's fate was sealed.

The next day his trial was held before a jury presided over by the Marquess of Montrose. A unanimous verdict was returned. Argyll was found guilty of treason and leasing-making but cleared on the count of perjury. The Privy Council then at once informed King Charles, requesting his agreement to the sentence of death and forfeiture upon the prisoner.[4]

*

The Duke of York, as his brother's representative in Scotland, was now doing all that he could to expedite the death and ruination of the man to whom he had borne a personal spite since his insistence on the addition of a clause against Roman Catholics in the Test Act. York himself insisted that all he intended was to rob Argyll of the hereditary rights to which Lauderdale (and the king) had restored him, and thus break his power over the Highlands.

Argyll himself, however, was convinced that York would stop at nothing to get rid of him. A friend, who was not named, overheard York say that 'the thing must be done, and that it would be easier to satisfy the king about it after it was done, than to obtain his leave for doing it.'[5] This seemed the more likely in view of the fact that Argyll's own father had been executed before the death warrant, signed by Charles II in London, had actually reached Edinburgh.

Argyll had a presentiment that such a fate would be his when, on the following Monday, 19 December, word reached him in the castle that the messenger, sent by the Privy Council to London, was expected back in Edinburgh in three days' time. Even more threatening was the news that the Justiciary Court would assemble to pass sentence immediately on the messenger's return. Argyll became even more certain of his impending fate when the Duke of York, by refusing to grant him an interview, made it plain that he was doing so in accordance with the rule that the king, or his representative, did not receive anyone under sentence of death.

This assumption was verified when, on the Tuesday morning, he heard that a large number of soldiers had been brought into Edinburgh. More menacing still, he learned on the following day that he was to be taken to the Tollbooth, the common jail, a clear indication of his impending execution.

The friends who were allowed to visit him urged him to try to escape but, undecided, he demurred. Then the messenger whom he had sent to London, after riding hard both day and night, reached Edinburgh, beating the envoys sent by the Privy Council by twenty-four hours. The man brought him letters which decided him. He learned that he was to be sentenced to death, the execution being delayed at the king's pleasure. This, as he knew, was a license for York to kill him. With death now virtually a certainty, he finally made up his mind to escape.

CHAPTER 20

'A Tall, Awkward Country Clown'

———⟫●⟪———

We do not know where Countess Anna and her daughters were living during these days of what must have been almost intolerable strain. It seems reasonable to think that they were in Edinburgh. Most probably they were staying with friends or relations: possibly they were at Moray House on the Royal Mile. Argyll's first wife had been a daughter of the Earl of Moray. This, coupled with the fact that his father had watched Montrose being led to his execution from a window of Moray House suggests an alliance between the families.

Lady Sophia Lindsay, Argyll's stepdaughter, must have been in or near Edinburgh on Tuesday, 20 December, the day on which, when warned of his impending execution, he summoned her to his prison. It was already dark, being five o'clock in the evening, when a trusted man came with the message (obviously arranged beforehand) which she immediately understood. Told to 'come up at once to see him and to bring a page in livery to carry her train, and another servant with a lantern to light her on the way to the Castle and back home'[1] she knew at once that Argyll's life was in dreadful danger from which she alone could save him even at great risk to her own.

Having obtained permission to visit her stepfather, Sophia is known to have reached the castle at about eight o'clock in the evening. Argyll's Lodging in Stirling is thirty-nine miles from Edinburgh; Castle Campbell, near Dollar, scarcely less. Therefore, from either place, it would have been impossible for her to have reached Edinburgh Castle within the space of three hours.

All that is known for certain is that she reached the castle with two servants. One carried a lantern, the other, a page, 'a tall, awkward country clown of a boy, with a fair wig and his head tied up as though he had been engaged in a fray'[2], bore her embroidered train, the height of fashion at the time. Orders had been given for the guards to be doubled and for no persons to be permitted to leave the Castle without showing their faces. Nonetheless, Lady Sophia, with her attendants, the page with his uncouth appearance no doubt causing some merriment, were allowed to enter the room wherein Argyll was held.

Almost as soon as the door shut behind them she was stripping off the page's clothes and putting them on to her stepfather, whom they fitted quite well. Then, when her allotted half-hour was ended, she parted with a great show of tears from the supposed Earl of Argyll who, condemned as he was to execution, she would never see again.

Lady Sophia, still acting the part of being greatly distressed, walked from the prison slowly and with great dignity, her page holding her train while a gentleman of the Castle escorted her to the gate. Outside there was a nerve-racking moment when the sentinel at the drawbridge, 'a sly Highlander', looked hard at Argyll. But, even as he leered at him, Lady Sophia, with great presence of mind, switched her train out of his hands so that it fell in the mud. Then, lashing it across his face, she shouted 'Varlet! Take that for knowing no better how to carry your lady's garment.'[3]

The sentry, distracted by the fury of this apparent virago, stepped back in a hurry before she could turn her rage on him. Then he let them pass . . . Surprisingly, after this, the main guard did not stop them. The great gate was opened and the lower guard formed into a double line through which Lady

Sophia and her escort were allowed to pass. Then came a horrible incident when one of the guards who opened the gate took Argyll by the arm 'rudely enough and viewed him' but, taking him for a poor simple boy, who was screamed at by his ill-tempered mistress, he pushed him out of his sight.[4]

At the outer gate Lady Sophia found her own coach waiting. She was handed in by the gentleman from the castle while Argyll, still acting the misused lackey, jumped up behind as was his place. They rattled off through the darkness, the carriage lights glinting on the cobbles, until, on reaching the Weigh House, or custom-house, at the foot of Castle Hill, Argyll slipped quietly off the back of the carriage. Then, still in his slippers, he hobbled down the West Bow, through the Grassmarket and Candlemaker Row and out at Bristo Port.

Here, to his intense relief, his horses were waiting as had been prearranged. The man holding them, who was to travel with him, held out dry stockings and riding boots but Argyll, although his feet were soaking from the mud and slush in the streets, did not stop to put them on. Riding knee to knee with his servant, who carried a lantern to show them the way, he reached a spot near Craigmillar Castle before he dared to draw rein. Then, with no sign or sound of pursuit, he discarded his soaking slippers – leaving them under a bush – and, pulling on the riding boots to which were strapped a pair of spurs, he rode as if all the devils were behind him, through the long hours of darkness to the south.

They were nearly two hours clear of the city before the moon, in her third quarter, rose at about eleven o'clock. Galloping through Dalkeith, they passed Newbattle Abbey, where Argyll had been born in 1629. From there they pressed on to Lauder, where the stronghold of Lauder Fort belonged to the Maitlands of Lauderdale, to whom, through her cousin Lord Lauderdale, Countess Anna was closely related. Here, after food and a short rest, they were given both fresh horses and a guide who was instructed to take them to a change-house at Torwoodlee, about two miles north of Galashiels.

From there Argyll sent his servant to the house of a Mr Pringle, a man whom he knew he could trust. Sure enough Pringle, on being given a password, clapped his hands with joy and at once ordered his own servant to saddle three horses, two for Argyll and his servant and one for himself. Pringle then went to the change-house, where, having embraced Argyll, he gave him all the gold he possessed. Then with his servant leading them, they set off across the border and into Northumberland, where, as Pringle assured them, they would find a Presbyterian minister who would, should it prove necessary, give them all that he possessed.

*

Argyll had escaped but Lady Sophia, his rescuer, was left behind to pay the price. The members of the Privy Council, incensed by what she had done to save him from imminent execution at their hands, wanted her to be scourged through the city of Edinburgh. However, the Duke of York forbade it, saying that 'they were not used to deal so cruelly with ladies in his country'.[5] She was nonetheless given a term of imprisonment, although evidence does not exist as to where she was held. Hopefully it was Edinburgh Castle, and not, as she was later to have to endure, the Tolbooth, the common, stinking, flea-infested jail. However, wherever she was held and whatever degradation she was forced to endure, Lady Sophia must soon have known that only her great courage had saved her stepfather's life.

It was very soon public knowledge that, just as Argyll had expected, the letter from the king granting the Privy Council's request for a sentence of death and forfeiture to be pronounced upon him, had reached Edinburgh on 21 December, only twenty-four hours after his hair-breadth escape from the castle.

In fact, the Court of Justiciary, in inflicting an act of forfeiture on Argyll, was acting illegally. Only parliament could pass such a sentence on a man not present in person to defend the charges made against him. Countess Anna submitted a petition to this effect but was completely ignored. Nonetheless the Privy Council, in this instance, acted with such blatant dishonesty that following the Revolution, the parliament of William III not only repealed Argyll's forfeiture, but authorised his son (the 10th Earl and 1st Duke) to bring a legal action against the judges who had so misused his father.

On 23 December, two days after the king's letter had arrived in Edinburgh, to the blowing of trumpets and the defacing of his coat of arms, Argyll's attainder was publicly proclaimed at the Market Cross.

Countess Anna was now the wife of an outlaw, denounced as a traitor to his king.

CHAPTER 21

He Rides Much in the Moonlight Mornings

On 24 December, three days after his escape from Edinburgh Castle, Argyll reached Stanton Hall in Northumberland, the home of the Reverend Mr Veitch. In Newcastle Mr Veitch bought three horses for £27. In his journal he recorded that he paid for them himself, Mr Hope, as Argyll now called himself, being short of money. Riding on together, they reached Leeds without incident and continued to Rotherham, where they put up at a Post House. Mr Veitch, having called for a flagon of ale and some wine, asked the landlord and his wife to come and join them. They were sitting at supper when a postboy appeared from Doncaster. He brought a letter for the landlord, which told him that a price of £500 was offered for Argyll's arrest. 'Dear Billy,' wrote his friend, 'if you find him and apprehend him in your road, let me go snips with you, and if I find him you shall go snips with me.' Mr Veitch, when shown the letter, roared with laughter and said 'Mr Hope here are admirable good news for you and me. The Earl of Argyll is escaped . . . we may come to hit upon him . . . and £500 reward will do us good service and bear our charges to London and back again; only I fear he rides much in the moonlight mornings.'[1]

He then told the landlord that he would give him a bottle of sack if he would allow his hostler to guide them to a village called Clown, on the border of Nottinghamshire. There they found an old Cromwellian, a Captain Lockyer, who offered to take Argyll safely to London. He proved to be as good as his word. When they reached Battersea, then four miles outside London, he took him to the house of a Mr Smith, a sugar baker, who was a very wealthy man.

Mr Smith, although financially successful, was an invalid, much dominated by his wife. This lady, Madam Smith as she was known, although 'very pious, wise and generous', was a martinet. A strict Presbyterian, passionately devoted to her creed, she exercised great influence in the network of dissidents scheming to overthrow the Anglican Church of England and to restore Presbyterianism in its place, as in the Commonwealth era. Told by Mr Veitch of Argyll's identity, she kept the secret to herself. Not even her husband, whose wits may to some extent have been failing, would she trust.

Initially, on his first arrival at their home in Battersea, Argyll was too physically exhausted to make a coherent plan. Thanks to Madam Smith, however, rooms were engaged for him as a Scottish gentleman called Mr Hope and for the Reverend Veitch, as a Captain Forbes, at some distance apart.

The arrangements were made by a Major Holmes, a friend of Madam Smith's who apparently knew Argyll. When told that the rooms were ready Madam Smith sent a servant with a lantern to guide her two visitors to Holmes' lodgings. Argyll, on entering his house, was surprised to be embraced by what appeared to him to be a perfect stranger. 'Pray Sir, where did you know me?' he asked, bewildered. Whereupon Holmes said 'My Lord, I knew you since that day I took you prisoner in the Highlands when you were Lord Lorne and brought you to the Castle of Edinburgh. But now we are on one side, and I will venture all that is dear to me to save you.'[2]

Argyll and Veitch then went to their separate lodgings, where they remained in hiding while the search to find them continued. Despite this the Earl of Shaftesbury somehow discovered the whereabouts of Veitch and summoned him to his presence. So secret was their meeting that they talked in Shaftesbury's bedroom, where Veitch, under questioning, admitted that Argyll was in London. Hearing this, Shaftesbury, having promised that he would not betray the fugitive, assured Veitch that he would do all in his power to help him.

Shaftesbury, the leader of the Whig party and Lord Chancellor from 1672–73, is now best remembered as the instigator of the Act of Habeas Corpus, a cornerstone of civil liberty, which he forced through the government in 1679. Despite his enlightened views, or more probably because of them, he was heartily disliked by the king, who called him 'one of the greatest rogues in England'.[3] Elsewhere described as 'the fair-haired villain'[4] he was the leader of a group of insurgents who aimed to destroy the monarchy. Arrested on a charge of high treason just before Argyll's arrival in London, he had only escaped with his life because the members of the jury assembled to try him had been supporters of his own party, then strongly influential in the city of London. Subsequently, as their lives and property were threatened by the Tory Royalists, both he and his confederates began plotting a series of risings throughout the country against the king.

*

Some time in the summer of 1662 Argyll had a meeting with Shaftesbury. While not committing himself to direct involvement in the politician's schemes, he advised him on the state of unrest amongst the Presbyterians in Scotland. He also told him bluntly that from his experience, the sum of no less than £30,000 sterling would be necessary to fund a successful rising. Later, however, after some argument, he agreed that £15,000 or even £10,000 might be enough to instigate a civil war.

The plans came to nothing, due, so it seems, to Shaftesbury's mistrust of Argyll. Meetings between those averse to the

English government, however, continued, in some of which Argyll was involved. An inn called the Dolphin, in Lombard Street, was a favourite rendezvous. Here it was that Argyll met his eldest son, Archibald, Lord Lorne, who, regardless of his father's forfeiture, was living, apparently quite openly, in London.

It was thanks to his son's connivance that Argyll, to his great joy, was reunited with his old friend Sir Arthur Forbes. It was now nearly thirty years since the day the two of them had kept a secret rendezvous in Kilchurn Castle to plan a revolt against Cromwell. Argyll, who was then still Lord Lorne, had then just sworn to his father that he would not converse with the Royalists. Together they had fought under Glencairn in 1653 before Argyll, after surrendering to General Monck, had saved Forbes' life by securing his release from Edinburgh Castle.

Following the Restoration, Sir Arthur, created Viscount Granard and a staunch Presbyterian, had become one of the two Lord Justices of Ireland.

Now, when they met in the Dolphin, the two spent several hours in deep discussion of the dangers threatening the Protestant religion and the state. Meeting again they agreed to join with the Duke of Monmouth 'and the honest nobility, gentry and commons in the three kingdoms that should appear for the Protestant interest'. Monmouth would head the projected rebellion in England, Argyll would do the same in Scotland, while Granard would send 5,000 seasoned troops from Ireland as reinforcements. Mr Veitch, who witnessed this agreement, remembered clearly how he then saw the two 'earls exchange walking sticks upon the contract'.[5]

*

In those days, however sent, letters were often opened. Because of this Argyll did not dare to risk any form of communication with his wife, or any of his family or friends in Scotland, for some time. However, as it became public knowledge, the punishment meted out to his stepdaughter, Lady Sophia, for aiding his escape lay most heavily on his mind. Two months after arriving in London he wrote to her, hoping that through the medium of poetry, he could somehow express his gratitude for all she had suffered for his sake.

18 April 1682

You came an angel in the case to me,
Expressly sent to guide and set me free.
The great gate opened of its own accord,
Then word came in my mind, I praise the Lord.

When I was out I knew not where I went,
I cried to God, and He new angels sent,
If ye desire what passed since to me,
Read through the book of psalms and think on me.

The noble friends I found here, greet you well,
How much they honour you it's hard to tell;
Or how well I am used, to say it all,
Might make you think that I were in Whitehall.

This seems to have been written when the search for Argyll had to some extent died down. So safe did he and Veitch now appear to be that Madam Smith took them both in her carriage out to Brentford, a village about seven miles from London, to a house she had just bought.

In this rural setting, Argyll, perhaps growing over-confident, walked about without disguise. Someone recognised him. This unnamed person, hoping to find favour or else financial gain, surreptitiously handed a note to Charles II, telling him that Argyll could easily be found. However, much to the disappointment of the informer, the king simply tore up the note and, throwing the pieces on the ground, exclaimed, 'Pooh! Pooh! Hunt a hunted partridge for shame!'[6]

Argyll was thus saved from immediate arrest. But his enemies were closing in. Next time the king, under their influence, might not be so magnanimous. Therefore, by means unrecorded, he managed to escape to Holland. Hardly had he left England than Lord Shaftesbury became his fellow refugee. A sick man, he survived a bare two months before dying on 21 January 1683.

PART 4

CHAPTER 22

The Rye House Plot

In Holland Argyll joined the band of Scottish refugees who were finding asylum in that country in increasing numbers. By the 1680s there were reckoned to be over 1,000 Scots in Rotterdam, renowned as it was as one of the largest trading centres in the world. The city was famous for religious tolerance, Holland being regarded as the most liberal society in Europe. It was now over forty years since a Scots kirk had been established in Rotterdam. This was partly due to the fact that Scottish and Dutch Calvinism were based on the same principles. The kirk was actually funded by the Dutch state, although spiritual guidance was still dictated from Edinburgh.

Despite the damage to trade caused by the two recent wars, relations between the two countries had been improved by the marriage of the Stadtholder, William, Prince of Orange (whose governess Countess Anna had been) to the Princess Mary, eldest daughter of James VII & II by his first marriage, to Clarendon's Protestant daughter, Anne Hyde. A treaty between the United Provinces of Holland and Great Britain had been signed on 29 January 1678.

Five years later, in the spring of 1683, Argyll, in Holland, sent a petition to Charles II asking that the sentence passed against him the previous year now be reviewed. He also asked for a safe conduct to London to allow him to have an interview with the king. Neither request received an answer. News from England then made it increasingly unlikely that the king would even contemplate a pardon, let alone grant an interview, to a man he knew to be involved with those who had plotted to murder him.

Word of a planned insurrection had been leaked to the government by the beginning of June. It was almost immediately followed by the discovery of the Rye House Plot, which, but for a fortunate accident, would have killed both King Charles II and his brother the Duke of York.

The ringleader of the plot was Richard Rumbold, an old Cromwellian and staunch republican nicknamed Hannibal, having only one eye. Despite his piratical appearance, he had married the rich widow of a maltster who lived beside the road to Newmarket in the aptly named Rye House. Rumbold's group planned to assassinate the king and his Roman Catholic brother as they returned from the races on the narrow stretch of road overlooked by his wife's house. Their scheme would almost certainly have succeeded but for the unforeseen incident of a fire at Newmarket, which caused the royal brothers to return to London a day earlier than planned. The perpetrators of the plot were betrayed and two of them, namely Lord Russell and Algernon Sidney, another former Cromwellian, were arrested, convicted of high treason and executed. A third, the Earl of Essex, a former member of parliament, committed suicide, greatly to the sorrow of the king. The Duke of Monmouth, who strenuously denied that he had had any intention of harming his father, nonetheless fled the country for Holland with a price upon his head. Received at the court of William of Orange, he immediately began forming plans for a campaign to make himself the Protestant King of England.[1]

Argyll's connection with the men who had conspired to kill the king and his brother was discovered by members of the government. On Tuesday, 26 June, Argyll's old friend Major Holmes (who had found lodgings for Argyll and Mr Veitch in London and whom Argyll had subsequently used as a courier for his correspondence with his wife and friends) was arrested and cross-examined by the king and the Privy Council. His home was searched, and his involvement with the conspirators was revealed when a large number of letters in cipher, with explanatory keys, was found. He confessed to having had correspondence with Argyll – a stalwart adherent of the Commonwealth, who detested the Royalist rule, Bishop Sprat called him 'Argyll's long dependent and friend'.[2] Someone, it seems, had betrayed him and when his house was searched the letters found included one from Argyll to Countess Anna, together with the key to its cipher.

Under interrogation Holmes revealed the name of another man, calling himself Mr Butler, who had arrived from the Continent only the day before. He told his inquisitors that the man was staying at an inn called the Pewter Pot, on the south side of Leadenhall Street. Here the unfortunate 'Mr Butler' was hauled from his bed in the early hours of the morning to be dragged before the king and Council and minutely questioned. He admitted that his real name was William Spence, that he came from a place called Sandreford in Fife but had recently been a student in Utrecht, claiming to have come to London to buy books. Asked if he knew the Earl of Argyll, he said he would recognise him if he saw him. Questioned then as to whether he had met the earl in Holland, he refused to answer. When he was shown one of the letters he said that he thought it to be in Argyll's handwriting but could not be sure. He swore that he knew nothing about its contents. The king, infuriated by this obdurate refusal to cooperate, ordered Spence to be imprisoned and held in irons. Taken to Edinburgh, he was tortured by 'the boots', a hideous contraption in which a man's legs were encased within frames lined with nails which were then tightened to penetrate the limbs. In agony, he did reveal the cipher in which Argyll's letter was written but clung to his insistence that he was ignorant, not only of the contents, but of the details of the Rye House Plot.

Holmes, an elderly gentleman of military bearing, suffered even greater torment and was eventually brought to trial. On the orders of the iniquitous Judge Jefferies, he was condemned to death and executed, his body being hung in chains.

The letters and documents found in Major Holmes' possession were immediately sent to the Privy Council in Edinburgh. When the Council met on 18 December 1683, the letter from Argyll to his wife was produced to immense excitement. Here at last, it was presumed, was proof in Argyll's own hand of his involvement in the Rye House Plot. The tension increased to a state of near hysteria amongst some of those crammed into the court as Countess Anna was summoned peremptorily to the bar of the Council.

Now over sixty, she entered, straight-backed and dignified as ever, refusing to give those ogling to get a better view of her the satisfaction of seeing her show even the slightest tremor of fear. The gabble of voices rose to a crescendo, then suddenly dropped to hushed silence as, turning to face those accusing her, she waited for the questions to begin. The Council then:

> remitted to the Lords Chancellor, Treasurer, and Duke of Hamilton, to speak with the Lady Argyll anent the deciphering of her letter to the late [forfeited] Earl of Argyll, her husband, and to report to them in that matter upon oath. The Council then remitted to the Earl of Perth, the Lords Register and Advocate, to tell her of her danger if she refused to do so, and these lords having also spoken with her, and reported that she was willing to depone, the Council remitted to the Earl of Perth to examine her upon oath, and communicate the result of her examination to the Lord Chancellor and Treasurer in the afternoon.[3]

Summoned again on the morning of 20 December, Countess Anna was first made to swear, with her hand on the Bible, that she would speak nothing but the truth. She was then closely questioned by the earls of Perth and Tweeddale, to whom she acknowledged that she had corresponded with her husband. This was illegal, he being a condemned traitor. However she confounded her husband's enemies with the plain-spoken honesty of her defence. She explained to them that 'for a long while past, ever since her husband's difference with the Mac-Leans about the island of Mull, when his correspondence had been similarly intercepted, he had been accustomed to write to her and to his friends even of his private affairs in cipher, and to that cipher she had a key. But upon the breaking out of the English plot, judging such a way of correspondence dangerous and liable to suspicion, she burnt it four months ago; and she cannot read nor expound them'.[4] Firmly, and in an unwavering voice, she declared that: 'all the letters she got contained nothing of the plot, but anent his own private affairs and his friends; and it would be a cruel law if a wife was obliged to detect and reveal these'.[5]

Her inquisitors, unsatisfied with her answers, then hastily sent for two men known to be skilled in interpreting hidden ciphers. One was Mr George Campbell, a resident of the Canongate in Edinburgh. The other a Mr Gray of Crechie in Angus. The Council, meanwhile, 'continued the advising of the oath until their next meeting, and the Earl of Balcarres was desired that the lady [his mother] might be in readiness at any time, when she should be hereafter called for'.[6]

The two code-breaking experts contrived to decipher the letter assumed to concern the plot and which had been the cause of such intense speculation. The breakthrough came when Spence, under duress, revealed that it was based on the number 128. Written in one hundred and twenty-eight horizontal lines, it consisted of eight columns of separate words. Then each of these was copied out vertically, so that the second word in the first sentence of the letter was in the hundred and twenty-ninth place after the very first word. To make it even more complicated, some words and phrases of importance were indicated by numbers such as 33, 69 etc., while countries such as England and Scotland were indicated as Birch and Brand.

The letter, purporting to be a business agreement, began with an introduction in plain English, which informed the reader that Mr B would explain matters and would also pay the sum of 128 guilders and 8 stivers, an intimation of how the lines and columns could be translated. The hopes of the inquisitors rose when they thought that some of the capital letters, with figures above them on the right hand, referred to the Earl of Balcarres, Anna's son. Thus, on 1 January 1684, they summoned her again. This time she managed to convince them that 'the symbol in question was only a relative particle in the key between her husband and her'. D 43, she told them, stood for the relative pronouns *he, his* or *him*. On the strength of this, suspicion of involvement in the Rye House Plot then fell upon Argyll's son-in-law Lord Maitland, husband of his daughter Anne. Richard, Lord Maitland, was in London but his father (who, on the death of his brother, had become Lord Lauderdale) was immediately summoned by the Council. Richard was then ordered to return home, accompanied by their clerk, Sir William Paterson and a Captain Patrick Graham, who were instructed to interrogate all the servants upon oath. Further to this they were then to place all the papers, trunks and cabinets of his son within a room where both door and windows were sealed, until they had been examined.[7]

However, despite a minute inspection of all his effects, no evidence incriminating Lord Maitland was ever found. Finally Anna was able to prove that the code in which the letter in question had been written was different from the one in which she and her husband had corresponded. Only three people knew of the cipher used in the letter which was acknowledged by Countess Anna to be in her husband's handwriting, and she was not one of them.[8]

The following is the alphabetical key which opened Countess Anna's letter from her husband. She had claimed to have destroyed it but either a copy was kept or she rewrote it from memory. The cipher used by Argyll in his explanation of his intended plans for a rebellion in Scotland, even if in some respects similar, was nonetheless essentially different.

	a b c d e f g h i j k l m n o p q r s t u v w x y z &
Alphabet 1st	10 11 12 13 14 15 16 17 18 19 20 21 22 23 24 25 26 27 28 29 30 31 32 33 34
,, 2nd	40 41 42 43 44 45 46 47 48 49 50 51 52 53 54 55 56 57 58 59 60 61 62 63 64
,, 3rd	70 71 72 73 74 75 76 77 78 79 89 81 82 83 84 85 86 87 88 89 90 91 92 93 94[9]

William Spence, now known to be Argyll's secretary, was told by his friends that the contents of the decoded letter were already known to the government and that nothing that he could say could bring further harm to his employer or to Countess Anna and finally made a declaration. He confirmed that over the previous two years a rebellion had been planned specifically to prevent the accession of the Roman Catholic Duke of York, the future James VII & II, in the event of his brother's death. The aim of those involved in the conspiracy was primarily to protect the Protestant faith and the constitutional liberties of the people.

The letter, which he had deciphered, had actually been sent from Holland on the day before Charles II had discovered the Rye House Plot, on 12 June 1683. Argyll, having given details of the way in which the rebellion was to be organised in both Scotland and England, complained both of the lack of money awarded to his scheme, and of the reluctance of known Protestant landowners to contribute men, horses and arms. He affirmed that he could control the whole of Scotland if given the money and soldiers he needed. Declaring that while he had kept the estimated costs of the projected civil war as low as possible, he was quite willing to submit his calculations to be examined by excellent advisers, whose verdicts he would subsequently accept. In conclusion, he wrote that he was so anxious to confer with associates in England that he would travel over there in disguise unless an envoy could be sent out to Holland. 'There were many things necessary to be done but which he dared not write down for fear of their coming to the knowledge of the enemy and putting them upon their guard.'[10]

Shortly before being induced to make his statement, William Spence had been forced to endure yet another form of torture: being goaded into staying awake for five days and nights. This, however, he had somehow survived, while his guards collapsed from exhaustion. Briefly imprisoned in Dumbarton Castle, on its rock in the estuary of the Clyde, he somehow managed to get free, whereupon he rejoined Argyll in Holland in 1684.

CHAPTER 23

Time Ripe for Rebellion

————➤●◀————

Countess Anna, at this time, lived largely in Argyll's Lodging in Stirling. Now, as when an exile in Holland, she had very little money. Her own small income of 4,000 merks a year, amounting to about £222 sterling, came from the estate of Wester Pitcorthie, near Balcarres, which was part of her first marriage settlement.

Shortly after Argyll's escape from Edinburgh Castle, the sum of 7,000 merks a year (about £388 sterling) had been allowed to her from the income of rents of his forfeited lands. King Charles, in remembrance of the Earl of Balcarres' loyalty to himself, and of the hardships Countess Anna had endured both before and after his death, had ordered the commissioners of the estates to give her precedence over all other creditors. Nonetheless, Argyll's lands were so impoverished that by April 1684 she had received only 4,600 merks of the 9,000 which she was due. Later, a petition to the Privy Council produced another 2,400 merks, but this was barely enough to live on, let alone to maintain even a skeleton staff. Indeed, so great was her poverty that she had once again to part with her personal possessions, just as she had thirty years before, in 1653, when she'd helped pay for Balcarres' army. Even her precious porcelain pots had to be sold. Nevertheless, it was only her own things with which she parted. Nothing belonging to her husband would she allow to be moved. Furniture, carpets and hangings were left for his return which, with her customary courage and optimism, she convinced herself and others would surely happen eventually.

Argyll's children were provided for out of their father's forfeited estate. Lord Lorne was denied possession of Inveraray but a sum of £1,250 sterling was settled on him. John, his partially disabled son was – probably for this reason – given £200 sterling a year, his brother's allowance being only £150 sterling. His sisters, however, with only £100 each, were nearly starving. Lady Jean was reduced to such penury that her cousin Lord Lothian married her, 'purely out of principle of honour, believing they suffered wrongly'.[1]

*

Meanwhile, across the North Sea in Holland, Argyll was himself in great financial difficulty. The income from his estates had vanished with their forfeiture. Only at the end of 1682 did he receive a gift of £50, collected from his tenants in Islay and Kintyre, who were poor enough themselves.

Some of his friends, however, were forthcoming with gifts of money. Foremost amongst them were the Smiths, that enigmatic couple who had found him lodgings in London, it would seem at their own expense. Madam Smith appears to have been infatuated, not only with the aim of overthrowing the existing government and establishing Presbyterianism in England, but also with Argyll himself. It is hard to reason otherwise in view of the fact that, when the earl fled London, she persuaded her husband (over whom she seems to have had complete control), to follow him, taking her with him.

Argyll, in the meantime, was living on a small estate in Friesland. The story runs that his father had bought it after a Highland soothsayer had told him that he would one day be driven from Inveraray. The land, lying close to a village called Oudwoude, near Leeuwarden, had thus belonged to his family for some time. This was his main base but he made frequent visits to Amsterdam and Rotterdam as well as to Utrecht, where he stayed with the ever-generous and hospitable Smiths.

The death of King Charles II on 6 February 1685 threw the conspirators in Holland into a fever of excitement. Faced with a Roman Catholic king in the brother who succeeded him, they determined that the time for rebellion had come.

From all existing evidence, it seems that it was Argyll's personal hatred of King James which fuelled his determination to rise in rebellion against him. The king, so Argyll stated, would never be at rest until he had stripped him of fortune, rank and perhaps of life.[2] Convinced that delay would only strengthen the new king's position, he made his views clear to the Duke of Monmouth through Spence who had resumed his employment as the earl's secretary.

Monmouth, who joined Argyll in Rotterdam, agreed that immediate action was imperative before the 'Duke of York', as he called his uncle, should have time to establish his predominance in Britain. Money, as ever, was a problem but Argyll was able to assure him that, through the generosity of his friends, of whom the Smiths were amongst the leading donors, he had been able to find £10,000 to pay for arms, ammunition, provisions and a frigate.[3] He also claimed, with great confidence, that he was assured of strong support in Scotland where, in his own former territory alone, he knew that he could raise an army of 5,000 men.

On hearing this, Monmouth, who was unsure of the strength of his support in England, offered to sail with Argyll to Scotland. Argyll was horrified, realising all too correctly that Monmouth, who had been commander-in-chief in both England and Scotland, could not act as his subordinate. The problem was solved at a meeting with Monmouth where it was agreed that simultaneous risings in both England and Scotland were absolutely essential to the plan of attack.

Monmouth would therefore lead a force of invasion into England while Argyll would do likewise in Scotland.

This settled, Argyll's preparations continued, but it was noticed by all those concerned that, renowned though he was for his short temper, he was now in a state of acute nervous tension which resulted in outbursts of rage. Suffering from what appears to have been persecution mania, he believed there was no one he could trust. Rotterdam had become dangerous. People had long ears. The town was full of spies. He therefore persuaded the conspirators to move to Amsterdam, where their final preparations were made.

CHAPTER 24

Secret Meeting in Amsterdam

⟶➤●◄⟵

Argyll was correct on one point. His plans were betrayed. Word sent secretly to Scotland robbed him of any chance to achieve victory by surprise.

The Privy Council, informed by secret agents that Argyll meant to invade the west coast, instructed the Marquess of Atholl (created Lord Lieutenant and Sheriff of Argyll) to hold the county in subjection by force of arms. Atholl's expenses, although considerable, were met by 'the gift and tack of the houses, parks and mill of Inveraray'. In addition, part of Argyll's forfeited lands were assigned for this purpose by the Crown.[1]

Atholl wasted no time. Marching to Argyllshire with an army about 1,000 strong, he seized Argyll's charter chest and papers, many of them stuffed into barrels in an attempt to hide them, and sent them from Inveraray Castle to the Privy Council in Edinburgh. All those even under suspicion of being in league with the rebels, including six of the 'indulged' ministers, were imprisoned. Argyll's eldest son, Lord Lorne, escaped from Inveraray Castle almost under Atholl's nose. Lord Neil Campbell, Argyll's brother, was only set free when he promised to abide by the laws of the government and to make all others do the same.

*

As ever in Scotland, when events of great portent were about to happen, strange manifestations began to be seen and heard.

Just as nearly thirty years before, when the Marquess of Argyll made his fatal visit to London, the dogs at Rosneath had set up a terrible howling, now, in December 1684, a shower of blue bonnets was seen in the air above Glasgow. At Moffat there was a cascade of blood, while at Rosneath, on the Gareloch, where the Marquess of Atholl had placed a garrison of fifty men, a little ghost appeared to beat the soldiers and tell them to make good use of their time because it would not be long.[2]

Argyll, in Holland, realised that he now had to contend with enemy garrisons within his own castle, in the heart of his own land. Nevertheless, undaunted, he went ahead with his plans. Three ships were purchased, two named after his wife and stepdaughter. The *Anna* carried thirty guns, the *Sophia* only six. The third, called the *David,* had ten. Loaded with arms, ammunition and stores, they lay at anchor, waiting for instructions to put to sea. Argyll had promised that they would be given only twenty-four hours' notice, both as to when they would sail and where they would land in Scotland.

On Friday, 17 April 1685, a meeting was held at Amsterdam; the twelve people gathered there included Argyll's third son, Charles. Sir John Cochran (the second son of Lord Dundonald) presided, and named the reasons for the forthcoming expedition: 'To declare and undertake a war against the Duke of York, for restoring and settling the true religion and the rights and liberties of the three kingdoms; to add to the Council of management on coming to Scotland such persons as might join them and be judged suitable thus to be associated with them; to choose the Earl of Argyll to be their general, "with a full power as was usually given to generals by the free states in Europe" and to appoint a person to draw up the declaration of war, to be given in at their next meeting.'[3]

Among those who went with Argyll on this invasion of Scotland were several who had been involved with him in the past. One was William Spence, his secretary. Another was

William Blackadder, son of the famous Nonconformist minister who had preached at a conventicle on the Craig of Balcarres. Described as 'a graduate in medicine in the University of Leyden', he was in fact the elder brother of the young man so stoutly defended by Lady Sophia when a prisoner in Stirling Jail. Others who sailed with Argyll included his two younger sons, John and Charles, Sir John Cochran and Sir Patrick Hume. The latter was a difficult and argumentative man, who later, as Lord Marchmont, was to be Lord Chancellor of Scotland. Amongst Argyll's less reputable companions were a Colonel Ayloff, nephew by marriage to the now deceased Lord Clarendon, and his notorious friend Colonel Rumbold, the one-eyed 'Hannibal' who, with a price on his head, was wanted in England as the instigator of the Rye House Plot. Most infamous of all were John Balfour of Kinloch and George Fleming, two of the murderers of Archbishop Sharp.

On Tuesday, 28 April, the long vigil ended at last. The little company left Amsterdam to sail north to board the waiting vessels at the Vlie, a passage then much used from the Zuyder Zee to the North Sea before the building of the North Sea Canal. On arrival they found that one of the three vessels, the *David*, was ready to sail. However, two days then went by while the *Anna* and the *Sophia* were loaded from lighters lying at anchor close by. Hardly was this completed before those on board saw, to their horror, that a man whom they recognised by his uniform as the English Consul, accompanied by others with telescopes, was repeatedly sailing round them. Messages were plainly being sent ashore before the consul and his companions set off by sea, heading towards Amsterdam. This could only mean that the consul intended to get orders from the States General to seize the ships of the expedition. Fortunately, however, before this could happen, the loading of the *Anna* and the *Sophia* was completed and the two ships were towed down the passage to the North Sea. Flags were then run up to the mastheads as signals for the customs officers to come on board.

There followed a long wait. Argyll, convinced that the English Consul already had orders to arrest them, paced the deck in a fever of impatience. He wanted to make a run for it but it was pointed out to him that, should his ships put to sea without being officially cleared, they would almost certainly be blown to pieces by the guns of the frigate lying at the mouth of the channel. Nearly mad with apprehension, he was forced to wait until at last the officials appeared. Passports and the ships' papers being found to be all in order, the three ships, ostensibly trading vessels bound for Venice, then received permission to depart. The Scottish soldiers on board hid below decks but, as they put into the North Sea, a yacht appeared in pursuit. Later Argyll was to hear that, chartered by the Dutch magistrates, who had become suspicious, she carried orders for them to return. A shot from one of his ships, however, sent the yacht scurrying back to port. The voyage from Holland to Scotland had begun.

CHAPTER 25

Invasion of Argyll

The three ships, carrying no more than 300 men, had a fair wind across the North Sea. Arriving off the Moray Firth in a gale, it was thought unwise to stay there for fear of being trapped on a lee shore, unable to put out to sea. Therefore they headed for the north of the mainland of Orkney. Somewhere near the islands the mist came down. Totally lost, they drifted through dangerous reefs until they found themselves in Scapa Flow, the channel, so notorious for its danger to shipping, which divides the mainland of Orkney from the island of Hoy. The fog was still thick but they could just discern the mainland, at sight of which William Spence, now the earl's chamberlain as well as his secretary, announced that he had an uncle in Kirkwall. Argyll let him go to find his relation and, more importantly, to bring on board a pilot who could guide them in safety through the currents and jagged rocks. However, this plan went badly wrong. Spence and William Blackadder did find their way to Kirkwall, only to be promptly arrested by Murdoch MacKenzie, the Bishop of Orkney who, warned by the Privy Council of a likely invasion, had put the town in a state of defence.

Argyll, on the advice of Sir John Cochran, sent a longboat manned by fifty armed men to find hostages for exchange. They seized several men of substance including James Stewart, the Laird of Graemsay, a descendant of the Stewart Earl of Orkney, a natural son of King James V. However, Argyll's suggestion that an exchange of prisoners should be made was treated with scorn by the bishop, secure in the knowledge that without heavy artillery no one could lay siege to Kirkwall with any hope of success. The hostages therefore remained prisoners on one of Argyll's ships.

Leaving Scapa Flow, through the perilous passage between the islands of Hoy and South Ronaldsay, the little fleet of invasion sailed into the Pentland Firth. From there, heading south through the Minch to the east of the Western Isles, the three vessels entered the Sound of Mull. The ships then anchored in the safe bay of Tobermory, a place familiar to Argyll. Here, twenty years previously, he had directed a search for the wreck of a ship of the Spanish Armada but had found, to his great disappointment, only a few rusty cannons instead of the fabled hoard of gold.

It was only six years since 1679, when, having proved his right of possession thanks to debts owed by the MacLeans of Duart, he had finally received a charter of possession of Mull from Charles II. Now, as an outlaw, he was returning to the island, which, like the rest of his lands, on the mainland and in the isles, was forfeited to the Crown.

*

Unknown to her husband, Countess Anna had also been in Argyllshire. Summoned by her daughter, Lady Henrietta, who had sent a message that she was ill, Anna had hastened, most probably from Stirling, to Carnasserie Castle at the head of Kilmartin Glen. The journey cannot have been easy, although Argyll was then at its loveliest, primroses smothering mossy banks, larks singing their hearts out to the sky. Anna could hardly have imagined that the land through which she travelled so peacefully would soon be torn apart by civil war.

Countess Anna arrived on that spring day to find not one, but both of her daughters in the castle. Lady Sophia had already gone to help her sister, who besides being of a nervous disposition evidently had poor health. Their mother, practical as ever, persuaded both of them to return with her to Stirling where, with its proximity to Edinburgh, the best doctors in Scotland could be found. As they departed, with Henrietta's little son Jamie, they were not to know that the castle they left behind them was soon to be full of armed men. Countess Anna returned to Stirling unaware of the advance of her husband's army and of the peril in which she and her daughters, particularly Sophia (who had organised Argyll's escape from prison), now stood.

*

On Monday, 11 May, Argyll anchored his ships in Tobermory Bay. Knowing only too well that, thanks to the resentment of the MacLeans, he would find little support on the island of Mull, he immediately sent his son Charles across to the mainland of Lorn with letters to his former vassals asking them to call out their men.

Charles was initially successful, taking the great fortress of Dunstaffnage, on the south shore of the entrance to Loch Etive. However, when he sent out his father's missives he met with crushing disappointment. In all, only an estimated 200 men rallied to the summons, while later it was to emerge that some who received Argyll's letters actually acted as traitors, sending them on to the Privy Council, while declaring themselves willing to join the Marquess of Atholl in his headquarters at Inveraray.

Still unaware of this betrayal, Charles crossed the hills to the great inland waterway of Loch Awe. Heading further west, he saw before him the towering and apparently impregnable fortress of Carnasserie, from which, unknown to him, his stepmother Countess Anna and his two stepsisters, one his beloved Sophia (to whom he was shortly to become engaged), had so recently left for Edinburgh. Having installed a garrison at the castle he rejoined his father, most probably at Crinan. Argyll, having sailed from Mull, is known to have anchored in the Sound of Islay, on Friday, 15 May. Once again Charles was sent ashore. Islay belonged to the Campbells of Calder (or Cawdor, as it was later spelt) but significantly they held it from the Crown, and thus were not vassals of Argyll.

At one o'clock in the morning of Sunday, 17 May, Charles, with a party of about 100 soldiers, landed on Islay. Hardly was he ashore than he found that he had been forestalled. Atholl had sent a detachment 450-strong to force the island-ers to swear loyalty to the king and to seize all the arms that they could find. To Argyll's enormous disappointment, only eighty men joined him. Calder, the 'Baillie' of Islay, had just given his word to the authorities in Edinburgh that, under no circumstances whatever, in the event of the rebels landing on Islay, would he give them any support. Even Argyll's threat to hang him if he did not produce 300 men left him entirely unmoved.

Thus chagrined, and seething with anger, Argyll crossed the Sound of Jura to Kintyre. On 20 May he landed at Campbeltown where, at the town cross, he made his Dec-laration of his reasons for raising a rebellion against King James VII & II.

*

Early in May the Privy Council, warned already by the Bishop of Orkney of the approach of Argyll's little fleet, had received intelligence that he was now off the west coast. Officers had been sent at once to Stirling where, in Argyll's Lodging, they arrested Countess Anna and her daughter Lady Sophia. Imprisoned first in Stirling Castle, they had then been taken to Edinburgh on the Sabbath morning of 10 May. Countess Anna was held in the Castle for five or six weeks. Meanwhile poor, courageous Sophia was thrown into the Tolbooth, the flea-infested, filthy common jail.[1] There, because of the part she had played in helping Argyll escape four years before, she was subjected to special hardship. Argyll's brother, Lord Neil Campbell, and James, his fourth son, were also arrested, but neither of them endured the cruelty imposed upon Lady Sophia.

Meanwhile, as both his wife and his stepdaughter suffered for his cause in Edinburgh, Argyll sent out the fiery cross, the *crois tara*, to all his former tenants in Kintyre. These farmers, staunch Presbyterians almost to a man, rallied loyally to his standard, giving him cause to believe that he would find strong support in the Lowlands, stronghold of the Presbyterian Church. Confirmation came from a minister, the Reverend George Barclay, who sent word that the enemy were panic-stricken. Monmouth had landed in England. The people of Ayrshire and Galloway were ready to rise against King James.

The news caused enormous excitement in Campbeltown, where Sir John Cochran wanted to take half of the army over to his homeland of Ayrshire immediately. Argyll nonetheless insisted that the men on his ships and his land forces should converge upon Tarbert, with its castle and natural harbour on the isthmus dividing Knapdale from Kintyre.

Here, on 27 May 1685, Argyll was joined by his son Charles and Henrietta's husband, Sir Duncan Campbell of Auchinbreck, with about 1,200 men. His army, including the 300 who had come with him from Holland, was now about 2,000-strong. He wished fervently to attack Inveraray, where the town and his own castle were held by Athollmen. It was, however, pointed out to him most forcibly that in doing so he would be sailing into a deathtrap. The English warships, known to be lying off the coast, could pursue and destroy his little fleet if it were hemmed in at the head of Loch Fyne. Argyll, much annoyed, then vacillated, constantly changing his mind until Sir John Cochran, in sheer desperation, said that he would land on the Ayrshire coast if only with a hayfork in his hand.

Eventually, because of a shortage of provisions, the army crossed over to Bute, the horses being transported in large, flat-bottomed boats. The Highlanders, at the sight of fat cattle, at once rounded up a large herd of beasts which they drove into Rothesay where, to their fury, they were forced by their commanding officers to return them to their owners. The earl's son, Charles, who was amongst the cattle 'lifters', was strongly reprimanded by his father. In disgrace, he was given a chance to redeem himself by being sent over to Cowal in command of 100 men, on a recruitment drive. From there, after being attacked and defeated by a party of Athollmen, he returned much dejected, having lost several of his men. It must have been shortly after this that Charles, on another recruiting expedition, was captured by a party of Atholl's soldiers. Although he was ill with a fever, his captors showed him no mercy, declaring that they were going to hang him in front of his father's castle at Inveraray. Before this atrocity could be carried out, however, the Marquess of Atholl saved him by asking the Privy Council to have him conveyed to Edinburgh. A letter written by Charles, while still in prison under the threat of death, thanked him for his kindness at this crucial moment.[2]

Argyll was then so furious to learn that his castle of Carrick, near Lochgoilhead, had been burnt, that he ordered that part of the old castle of Rothesay, long inhabited by the early Stewart kings, should also be destroyed by fire. On word of

English men-of-war approaching, he realised the danger of remaining on the island of Bute. He therefore crossed over to Cowal on the mainland, where he quartered his men near the largely ruined Toward Castle, another of his former properties, taken from the Lamonts but by now in the hands of the Crown.

From Castle Toward, on the north side of the Clyde, Argyll's ships sailed up the Kyles of Bute to the small castle of Ellan-Gheirrig, on an island in Loch Riddon. This fortress, held by the Campbells since the 1400s, was, so Argyll believed, totally impregnable from an attack from the sea. Convinced that the English ships, should they attempt pursuit, must inevitably run aground, he thought he had found a safe haven. But, as three frigates and a yacht cut off the entrance to the castle, he quickly realised his mistake. There could now be no escape by sea.

They could, however, reach the land . . . A detachment of the army, under Colonel Rumbold, marched north up Glendaruel and took the castle of Ardkinglass at the head of Loch Fyne. Driven out from there by a force of Athollmen from Inveraray, they then rejoined the rest of the army at the head of Loch Riddon.

Argyll left Ellan-Gheirrig on 11 June, the very day on which Monmouth landed at Lyme in Dorset. Much depressed by the desertion of many of his Highland men, he was nonetheless encouraged by Sir John Cochran and Sir Patrick Hume, who assured him that in the Lowlands he would find strong support.

Having crossed Loch Long from Ardentinny, the army lay on the east bank all night. But here they were joined by the men left behind to garrison Ellan-Gheirrig, who brought disastrous news. Firstly they had failed to obey Argyll's orders to sink the ships. Then the prisoners from Orkney, who had been left in the castle, had attracted the captains of the English frigates with some sort of white flag. A party of sailors, sent to rescue them, had burst into the castle just in time to extinguish the sizzling fuse leading to the gunpowder which would have blown the fortress apart. Barrels of explosives, a large stock of armaments, Argyll's precious standard and the hostages, all had been left behind in the garrison's rush to escape.

Distressing as this news was, the army continued down the shore of the Gareloch before crossing the river Leven, three miles north of Dumbarton.

It was now known that, while Atholl's men were pursuing from the north, the Earl of Dumbarton, a Roman Catholic who was Commander-in-Chief of the Royal army in Scotland, was before them, somewhere near Glasgow. For this reason Argyll did not take the direct route to the city but headed for Stirling, turning south near the village of Drymen to approach Glasgow through the Blane valley. Told that a detachment of the enemy had been seen on the highroad to Killearn, Argyll became very nervous but nonetheless gave commands that a camp be made near Duntreath Castle. Fires were lit, but hardly were they burning before orders were given to march to Glasgow, a distance of about twelve miles.

Local men had been found to act as guides but, in the darkness of a misty night, they got lost in the Kilpatrick Hills. In a house somewhere by the Clyde, most probably a local inn, Argyll asked Sir John Cochran for his advice on what to do. Cochran, who had only recently been so confident of support in Ayrshire, now realised that, in view of their recent disasters, Argyll's cause was virtually lost. His small force, inadequate even at the start of the campaign, had been steadily dwindling. Now, in daylight, it became evident that during the previous night many of the Highland men had seized the chance of vanishing into the mist. Argyll himself was physically exhausted and virtually prostrated with nerves. He was, as Cochran realised, in no fit state to command men, most of whom had lost confidence in him as a leader. Having rapidly assessed the situation, he told him bluntly to return to the Highlands 'for it is to no purpose for you to go over the Clyde'.[3]

Nonetheless Argyll, with the obstinacy of a man unclear of his own intentions, determined to stick to the plan made in Kintyre, of heading south into Ayrshire. Together with Sir Duncan Campbell of Auchinbreck, his younger son (the slightly disabled John), a Major Fullarton and a Captain Duncanson, he rode towards Glasgow. Then, as the Highland hills to the north-west became clear on the horizon, it was decided that Sir Duncan should make for his home country, while Argyll, Fullarton and his son would head into Renfrewshire over the Clyde.

Argyll, by now very nervous of capture, changed clothes with Fullarton's guide, donning the rough jacket and the blue bonnet which most countrymen wore. Reaching a ford about a mile from Renfrew, he was actually crossing the river when two of a party of militia men who were patrolling the bank rode into it and tried to pull him off his horse. Grappling with them, he fell off but, scrambling to his feet, he held them at bay with his pocket pistols.

Seeing them stumble back before him, their hands held above their heads, he believed he had escaped. Perhaps confused by his fall he then, most unwisely, tried to cross the Clyde on foot. The officer who commanded the soldiers, alarmed by a local man who had seen what had happened, sent two of his troopers to arrest the supposed country yokel who, surprisingly, appeared to be armed. Drawing their pistols they fired at him. The bullets fell short, but at this point a weaver called John Riddell, hearing the commotion, grabbed an ancient broadsword and ran out of his cottage nearby.

Riddell was drunk. Nonetheless he lunged at the unknown man in front of him, hitting him over the head with his sword. The earl, half-stunned, falling backwards into the water, murmured the fatal words, 'unfortunate Argyll'. Hearing him, the weaver, bemused as he was, recognised the identity of the man he had just attacked. Hardly had he become aware of it before another party of soldiers, commanded by Sir John Shaw of Greenock, a local laird, rode up to arrest the prisoner. Shackled and closely guarded, Argyll was taken on horseback to be delivered to the Earl of Dumbarton, Commander-in-Chief of the Royal army in Glasgow.

CHAPTER 26

Held at His Majesty's Pleasure

Argyll was held in the Tolbooth, most filthy and revolting of prisons. Here he was shortly joined by none other than Rumbold, main instigator of the Rye House Plot who, taken prisoner at Lesmahagow while trying to reach England, was dragged, badly wounded, to the jail. Later a man named John Hall, presumably possessed of some medical knowledge, was paid £55 2/ Scots by the Treasury for 'dressing the late Argyll, Rumbold (and others) the tyme they were prisoneris in the Tolbooth, being all wounded, and for furnishing drugs to them conform to the compt thereof'.[1] Rumbold, subsequently taken to Edinburgh, met his death at the hands of the executioner, 'with great resolution, declaring, almost on the scaffold, that he did not believe God had made the greater part of mankind with saddles on their backs and bridles in their mouths and some few booted and spurred to ride the rest'.[2]

On the same day that Argyll was arrested, Sir John Cochran, with about seventy men, the remnants of the small invasion force, did succeed in crossing the Clyde. However, he got only as far as Muirdyke, near Lochwinnoch in Renfrewshire, before encountering a strong Royalist force. Cochran's men fought fiercely but, being outnumbered, were rapidly overcome. Sir John, himself taken prisoner, had his life saved by his father, Lord Dundonald, who succeeded in bribing 'priests about the Court' to the tune of £5,000 sterling. Taken to London, Sir

John was questioned by King James, to whom he is said to have revealed much information.

Colonel Ayloff, related by marriage to King James' first wife, stabbed himself in his cell in Glasgow. He survived, but only to be taken to London for trial and execution. William Spence, Argyll's secretary, his death sentence reprieved, remained a prisoner until the accession of William III in 1689. Likewise Sir Patrick Hume, who found sanctuary in Holland, returned to be made Lord Marchmont and Lord Advocate of Scotland.

On 6 June, just twelve days before Argyll himself was captured, William Blackadder and William Spence had been taken by sea from Kirkwall, in Orkney, to the port of Leith. They arrived to hear that Blackadder's father, the Reverend John, had died on the Bass Rock, having been held prisoner there since 1681. William Blackadder, although interrogated and imprisoned by the Privy Council in Edinburgh, was spared execution thanks to the quick-witted action of his sister, who ripped incriminating papers from within the lining of his hat.

*

Lady Henrietta, Argyll's stepdaughter, hearing of the disaster to his army, was so frantic with worry for the safety of her husband, Sir Duncan Campbell of Auchinbreck, that, entrusting her little son (then about six years old) to a nurse, she set off to seek news of him. Leaving Argyll's Lodging, where she had lived since her illness, wearing a deep disguise and wrapped in a heavy cloak, she headed for Edinburgh, alternately leading and riding her horse. From this description it seems that she passed herself off as a countrywoman, probably a farmer's wife. Riding alone on an old nag she would certainly never have been taken for a lady of high rank.

At Falkirk, about twelve miles on her way, she caught up with a coach emblazoned with the arms of Lord Dundonald, conspicuous by its three boars' heads surmounted by the crest of a horse. Intrigued to know why such a grand equipage should be heading the same way as herself, she questioned some bystanders to learn to her utter horror and fear that it was carrying her stepfather, Argyll, to imprisonment. She followed as far as she was able but her old horse, outpaced by the coach team, seems to have gone lame and could go no further. She did, however, manage to reach Edinburgh the following morning where, to her enormous relief, she learned that her husband was alive and well.

Unknown to her he had changed his mind about going to the Highlands and was in Edinburgh. Seen and recognised in the Canongate, he ran for his life and managed to escape and hide in the city until, probably from Leith, he fled the country for Holland on the well-known route for refugees, over the North Sea.

Lady Henrietta then, in her own words, was 'more enabled to make inquiry after my dear afflicted mother, who was harshly treated: and seeing her under so great affliction by the approaching suffering of such an endeared husband (and had no access to him – although both were prisoners in the same castle – till eight days after this fatal stroke) this did again renew a very mournful prospect of matters, which at this time had a very strange aspect, so that if the Lord of life had not supported, we had sunk under the trouble.'[3]

On Saturday, 20 June, Argyll had been brought a prisoner into Edinburgh. On reaching the Water Gate, he had been met by a Captain Graham and given the option of walking or of riding in a cart through the Canongate to the Castle. On his choosing to go on foot, he was seen to turn pale as, with his hands tied behind his back, he was fastened by a rope round his waist to the hangman. After that, in near darkness, it being ten o'clock at night, he was taken as a common criminal, stumbling over the cobbles up the street where, only four years earlier, he had carried the crown in full regalia at the opening of the Scottish parliament in 1681.

CHAPTER 27

'It Can Only Be Termed a Judicial Murder'

Argyll, now a prisoner in Edinburgh Castle for the third time in his life, was held in the tower which still bears his name. Loaded with heavy iron shackles, which caused open sores to develop on his limbs, he was held under close supervision. The authorities were taking no chances of letting him escape, as when Lady Sophia had set him free.

We do not know in which part of the castle Countess Anna was held. The only evidence rests on the word of her daughter, Lady Henrietta, who wrote that, although they were in the same prison, her mother was only allowed to see her husband on the morning of his execution, eight days after the evening when he had been so ignominiously dragged into the Castle.

Argyll was in an invidious position. Sentenced to death for treachery for failing to subscribe entirely to the Test Act in 1681, he was in fact legally dead. For this reason he was now sentenced to execution on the original charge, the date and manner of his death being left to the discretion of the king. Meanwhile, on the orders of the Privy Council, he was frequently interrogated on all the details involving the rebellion, particularly on the names of those with whom he had been involved. James VII & II wrote to the Privy Council urging them to use torture if necessary to extract information.

Told of the king's orders Argyll merely said, 'I am to be put to the torture, if I answer not all questions upon oath; yet I hope God shall support me.' Then writing to Madam Smith in

Amsterdam, he said, 'I die upon mine old sentence, and nothing of what passed lately is to be in public on either hand. Your name could not be concealed, and I know not what any paper taken may say, otherwise I have named none to their disadvantage.'

Argyll did not give any evidence which could be used to bring those implicated with him to trial on a charge of treason. The threat of torture did not materialise, due, it would seem, to the time that it might involve. The king was determined that the execution must take place within three days.

*

From the time of his arrest the mental agony of Argyll's family and those close to him is easy to understand. Strangely enough, Argyll himself underwent a metamorphosis. Irascible by nature, he had been on the verge of what in modern terms would be described as a nervous breakdown during his failed campaign. Now, when events had moved beyond his control, he was calm in acceptance of his fate. His clarity of mind and complacency regarding what was to come is revealed in the eulogy which he wrote in his prison in the Castle, on the night before his death.

> Thou passenger, that shall have so much time
> To view my grave and ask what was my crime:
> No stain of error, no black vice's brand
> Was that which chased me from my native land.
> Love to my country, twice sentenced to die,
> Constrain'd my hands forgotten arms to try,
> More by friends' fraud my fall proceeded hath,
> Than foes: though now they thrice decreed my death.
> On my attempt though Providence did frown,
> His oppressed people God at length shall own.

Another hand by more successful speed,
Shall raise the remnant, bruise the serpent's head.
Though my head fall, that is no tragic story,
Since going hence I enter into glory.[1]

Lady Henrietta gives a poignant account of the following day, that of his execution:

The day being appointed for his suffering she [Countess Anna] had access to him, and, though under deep distress, was encouraged by seeing the bounty and graciousness of the Lord to him, in enabling him with great courage and patience, to undergo what he was to meet with. . . .

In that morning that his dear life was to be surrendered to the God that gave it, he uttered great evidence of joy that the Lord had blessed him with the time he had in Holland, as the sweetest time of his life, and the mercifulness of his escape to that end; but rejoiced more in the complete escape he was to have that day from sin and sorrow – yet in a little fell into some damp, and in parting with my mother was observed to have more concern than in any other circumstance formerly; which to her was a bitter parting, to be taken from him whom she loved so dearly. But in a little time after he recovered a little, and as the time of his death drew near, which was some hours after, the Lord was pleased wonderfully to shine on him to the dispelling of clouds and fears, and to the admitting him to a more clear and evident persuasion of his Blessed favour, and the certainty of being so soon happy – in which he expressed his sense in his last letter to my dear mother, which could not but sweeten her lot in her greatest sorrow, and was ground of great thankfulness that the Lord helped him to the last to carry with such magnanimity, resolution, contentment of mind, and true valour, under this dark-like providence to endless blessedness . . . He laid down his dear life June 30 1685. This morning liberty was obtained at length for my seeing him, but not till he was brought to the Council-house where I was enabled to go to him; when he had a composed edifying carriage, and after endearing expressions, said 'We must not part like those not to meet again!' and he went from thence with the greatest assurance.[2]

In the castle, dinner had been served to him before noon. Afterwards he had lain down and had his usual afternoon sleep, as had been his habit ever since the accident when playing at the 'bulletts' in the courtyard of the Castle during his first imprisonment there in 1658. The picture entitled *The Last Sleep of Argyll* by E.M. Ward, which shows him lying peacefully on a couch, hangs in the corridor of the House of Commons. The story runs that an unnamed official, who saw him through an open door, departed hysterical with grief, comparing his serenity with the turmoil of his own mind.[3]

The time came when the earl must forever leave the castle and go out to his execution; and he was accompanied with several of his friends down the street to the Laigh Council-house, where he was ordered to be carried before his execution. It was here, where he said goodbye to his stepdaughter, Lady Henrietta, that he showed an astonishing firmness of purpose as he calmly sat down to write his last letters. The first was to his wife:

Dear heart

As God is himself unchangeable, so He hath been always good and gracious to me, and no place alters it; only I acknowledge I am sometimes less capable of a due sense of it: but now, above all my life, I thank God, I am sensible of his presence with me, with great assurance of His favour through Jesus Christ; and I doubt not it will continue till I be in glory.

Forgive me all my faults, and now comfort thyself in Him, in whom only true comfort is to be found. The Lord be with thee, bless thee, and comfort thee, my dearest!

Adieu, my dear!

Thy faithful and loving husband,

Argyll[4]

His second letter was written to Lady Sophia, for whom he is known to have had a great affection.

My dear Lady Sophia,

What shall I say in this great day of the Lord, wherein, in the midst of a cloud, I find a fair sunshine. I can wish no more for you but that the Lord may comfort you and shine upon you as He doth upon me, and give you the same sense of His love in staying in the world as I have in going out of it.

Adieu!

Argyll

P.S. My blessing to dear Earl of Balcarres. The Lord touch his heart and incline him to His fear![5]

The third letter was to Lady Henrietta.

Dear Lady Henrietta,

I pray God to sanctify and bless this lot to you. Our concerns are strangely mixed – the Lord look on them! I know all shall turn to good to them that fear God and hope in His mercy. So I know you do, and that you may still do it more and more is my wish for you. The Lord comfort you! I am,

Your loving father and servant,

Argyll[6]

One more letter, apparently written earlier in the day, was afterwards discovered. It was addressed to his son, John, who had accompanied him on his expedition but who had taken no active part because of the malformation of his hands. John had escaped but was afterwards captured and held prisoner in Stirling.

Edinburgh Castle, June 30, 1685

Dear John,

We parted suddenly, but I hope shall meet happily in heaven. I pray God bless you, and if you seek Him, He will be found of you. My wife will say all to you; pray love and respect her. I am,

Your loving father,

Argyll[7]

The fate of John was uppermost in his father's mind even as he went to his death. In the Laigh Council-house he emphasised to those attending him that, because of his disability, John had never borne arms. He also pleaded for the safety of all his children and 'for the poor people who had been with him, his clansmen and vassals, as having been for the most part constrained to follow him in his late rebellion.'[8]

Lord Alexander Lindsay gives a moving account of Argyll's death:

After writing the preceding letters he proceeded to the place of execution. On reaching the midst of the scaffold, he took leave of his friends, heartily embracing some of them in his arms, and taking others by the hand. He delivered some tokens to the Lord Maitland [husband of his daughter Anne] to be given to his lady and children; then he stripped himself of his clothes and delivered them to his friends and, being ready to go to the block, he desired the executioner might not be able to do his office till he gave the sign by his hand; and falling down on his knees upon the stool, embraced the maiden (as the instrument of beheading is called) very pleasantly, and with great composure he said, 'it was the sweetest maiden ever he kissed, it being a means to finish his sin and misery, and his inlet to glory, for which he longed'. And in that posture, having prayed a little within himself, he uttered these words three times. 'Lord Jesus receive me into thy glory!' and then gave the sign by lifting up his hand, and the executioner did his work, and his head was separated from his body.[9]

Argyll died a martyr for his religion as embodied in the Presbyterian Kirk. Over 100 years later, Sir Walter Scott, himself a lawyer, was to write that: 'When this nobleman's death is considered as the consequence of a sentence passed against him for presuming to comment upon and explain an oath which was self-contradictory, it can only be termed a judicial murder.'[10]

CHAPTER 28

'God's Favour to That Family'

Following Argyll's death his widow, Countess Anna, and her daughter, Lady Henrietta Campbell, went immediately to England. They spent three months in Windsor and in London where, at the court of King James, they importuned for Henrietta's husband, Sir Duncan Campbell of Auchinbreck. Their purpose was to try and get him a pension, on the grounds that, as a loyal supporter of Charles II, he deserved some monetary compensation. The late king's brother, however, proved obdurate in his refusal to permit any kind of income to a man now labelled a traitor and living in exile abroad.

Defeated, Countess Anna returned to Scotland, while Henrietta journeyed to Holland to join her husband. Later, she returned to Scotland to collect little Jamie, their only child. Afraid of being arrested she wrote that, 'the times being troublesome', she came in heavy disguise to the house of a dear friend, Mr Alexander Moncrieff, 'where I had much kind welcome and sympathy'. Then she adds a rather charming tribute to her mother, Countess Anna, whose steadfast resilience in adversity during the tragic and trying circumstances of the last few months had held the whole family together.

But any uncertain abode I had was with my dear mother in Stirling, whose tender care and affection has been greatly evinced to all hers, and particularly to such as desire to have more of the sense thereof than can be expressed as the bounden duty of such; and I cannot but reckon it among my greatest earthly blessings to have been so trysted, having early lost my dear father, eminent in his day, when insensible of this stroke; and when so young, not two years old, and deprived of his fatherly instruction, it may justly be ground of acknowledgement that the blessed Father of the fatherless, in whose care I was left, did preserve so tender-hearted a mother, whose worth and examplariness in many respects may be witness against us if undutiful to the great Giver of our mercies.[1]

This letter from Lady Henrietta proves that immediately after Argyll's death, her mother was living at Argyll's Lodging in Stirling. Her son Colin, Earl of Balcarres, then mostly in London, was much about the court. It was he who persuaded the king to grant an annual pension of £800 sterling a year to Argyll's eldest son, now the 10th Earl, who was living in great penury since the forfeiture of his father's estates. This was justifiable; the young man, after a dramatic escape from Inveraray to Holland in 1685, had taken no part in his father's rebellion. Once allowed his pension, he went to Holland from whence he returned to Scotland when William and Mary were acclaimed joint sovereigns in 1689.

Subsequently he enjoyed a meteoric career. One of the three commissioners sent to offer the crown of Scotland to the new king and queen, he then, on 11 May 1689, administered the Coronation Oath. Shortly afterwards, by an act of the Scottish Parliament, his father's estates were restored to him and two years later, in 1701, he became the first Duke of Argyll.

*

In 1688, Countess Anna had shared in the happiness of her daughter Sophia when Charles Campbell returned from

Holland where he too had lived as a refugee. Charles, the third son of Countess Anna's late husband, Argyll, had fought alongside his father until taken prisoner by the Athollmen. Tried before the Justiciary Court and forfeited on his own confession, he had then been sentenced to banishment, never to return again (to Scotland) on pain of death. It is said that he was saved from execution by the pleas of 'several ladies who believed that he was married to Lady Sophia'.[2] He was in fact engaged to Sophia. They were married almost immediately on his return from Holland, but perhaps due to her age (she was already forty at the time) there were no children.

The year of 1688, as far as Countess Anna was concerned, proved to be one of extraordinary events. It was now nearly thirty years since, as a virtually penniless refugee in Holland, she had, through the kindness of Princess Mary, widowed sister of King Charles II, been given the position of governess to the son of the Stadtholder of the Netherlands. The little boy, frail and undersized as he was, had loved playing at soldiers. Now a man of forty-eight, he had proved himself a general of international repute in Holland's war with France. More importantly, as far as the people of Britain were concerned, he was also the husband of King James VII & II's eldest daughter, another Princess Mary.

It was during this momentous year of 1688, that, on 10 June, Mary of Modena, the Roman Catholic second wife of James VII & II, gave birth to a son. The young prince, christened James Francis Edward, was to live to be known as the 'Old Chevalier' or more commonly the 'Old Pretender'. At the time of his birth it was realised that, as a son, he would most likely override the claim of his Protestant half-sister, Princess Mary, to succeed to the throne of Britain and Ireland. This probability sent shock-waves through the largely Protestant populations of both England and Scotland. So strong, indeed, was the antipathy of the majority of influential people in England to the likelihood of another Catholic monarch that the Whigs and Tories in Parliament actually joined forces to invite Princess Mary and her husband, William, Stadtholder of the Netherlands, to come over to England to rule in her father's place.

Subsequently, on 5 November, William landed at Brixham in Devon with a large army, estimated as a combined force of 15,000 cavalry and infantry, many of whom were mercenaries from abroad. On 11 December King James made an abortive attempt to escape by boat. While doing so, he famously dropped the Great Seal in the Thames before being captured by fishermen near Sheerness, on the Isle of Sheppey. Returning to London, he was met with a message from William, his son-in-law, telling him to abandon the capital. Confronted with this ultimatum, King James fled to France as William entered London on 23 December.

Less than two months later, on 13 February 1689, William and Mary, who had been offered the throne by the Convention of Parliament, jointly acceded as king and queen. Their coronation, at Westminster Abbey, took place on 11 April, on which day the Scottish Convention of Estates declared that James VII & II was no longer King of Scotland. Shortly afterwards a delegation consisting of the Earl of Argyll for the lords, Sir James Montgomerie for the barons, and Sir John Dalrymple for the burgesses, carried the Convention's proposals to London together with the offer of the crown, terms which William and Mary accepted on 11 May.

Thus, in what must have seemed to her to be an act of just revenge, did Countess Anna learn that the man whom she held responsible for the brutal death of her second husband, Argyll, had himself been driven into ignominious exile by none other than the delicate child she had cared for, who was now King William II[3] of Scotland, and in England and Ireland, William III.

*

Lady Henrietta and her husband, Sir Duncan Campbell of Auchinbreck, lived in Rotterdam until the 'Glorious Revolution', which ended with the coronation of William and Mary in 1689. Although very impoverished, having no form of regular income, the Campbells were greatly helped by King William's parents, the Prince and Princess of Orange.

On Sir Duncan's sailing with King William to England, his wife witnessed their embarkation in a storm. To her horror she saw the ship driven back to the shore but afterwards, when she realised they had thus missed an encounter with a French squadron lying off the harbour, she believed that divine intervention had saved the lives of all on board. That night, with her husband safely returned, and the expedition postponed, she sailed with him to Helvoetsluys, only to find it almost impossible to get lodgings there, the place being crowded out with largely Scottish refugees. Eventually discovering somewhere to stay, they remained there until, on 1 November 1688, the expedition to England finally set sail.

When the Campbells of Auchinbreck returned home to Argyllshire they found that the vacuum of power left by the death of the late earl had resulted in a free-for-all. Neighbour fell upon neighbour, some rekindling old feuds. The Athollmen had taken everything they could lay hands on, from cattle down to household goods. Pots and pans, glass from the windows, rolls of cloth and even the minister's wigs had been purloined and stolen away. The Campbells had not been spared.

Argyll's son, Charles Campbell, when sent over to the mainland from Mull by his father in May 1685, had left a garrison in Auchinbreck's castle of Carnasserie. Some time towards the end of June in 1685 when Argyll, held prisoner in Edinburgh Castle, was awaiting the order of execution, it was reported from Inveraray that a force of 600 men had marched to attack Carnasserie, to which they were intending to lay siege. The Marquess of Atholl announced that 'it had been partly blown up by treachery'[4] but Sir Duncan, on his return, claimed that it had been besieged by MacLeans, led by MacLean of Torloisk who, vengeful of the loss of their island to the late Earl of Argyll, had sailed over from Mull. Joined by Sir Duncan's own neighbour, Archibald Maclachlan of Craiganterve, who also had an old score to settle, they had laid siege to the castle and, following its surrender, 'did barbarously murder Alexander Campbell of Strondour, Sir Duncan's uncle', wound about twenty of the garrison, steal sixty horses and 'did set fire to the said house of Carnasserie, and burn it to ashes'.[5] Sir Duncan claimed £20,000 Scots in compensation but did not restore the building, which was soon described as being in great need of repair.

The terms of capitulation had included an agreement that all the furniture and papers should be preserved, to be delivered to Lady Henrietta. These conditions were ignored. The 'commander of the party', presumably MacLean of Torloisk, took a great fancy to the charter-chest, which was of a unique design. Breaking it open, he threw all the papers on the floor and went off with the chest, while a party of his men remained in the house for over two months. Lord Alexander Lindsay, having described this, writes that, 'After the revolution, when Auchinbreck came home, that house was just ruined and open to everybody. He went not to it but to another.'[6] This second house was probably the castle of Kenlochgair, on the east shore of Loch Fyne. Plundered by the Athollmen in 1685, it must have been hastily repaired.[7]

From there Lady Henrietta insisted on going to Carnasserie to look for the papers, against the advice of her husband, who said they would all be destroyed. Entering the silent, blackened building, she found them just as they had been left when tipped from the charter-chest, lying in a heap on the floor. Packing them into trunks she then took them to Edinburgh, where, to everyone's amazement, it was found that nothing of importance was missing, which she said she thought 'was a token of God's favour to that family'.[8]

CHAPTER 29

Return to Balcarres

Countess Anna is known to have moved to Balcarres in 1689. From then on the old castle, where she had lived so happily with her first husband, was to be her permanent home. Once again, as on her return from Holland following Alexander Balcarres' death, she became the manager, or factor, of her son's estate.

She somehow contrived to settle outstanding debts although she herself was not at all well off. In the previous year of 1688, she had voluntarily relinquished her jointure of £7,000 per annum from the virtually bankrupt Argyll estates. Previous to this she had made over the pension of £1,000 a year, settled upon her and her two sons by Charles II, to Colin.

Colin, 3rd Earl of Balcarres, a man of thirty-six, was a member of the Scottish Parliament which convened on 14 March 1689. Despite the infidelity of James VII & II to his mother and stepfather he was one of the leading Jacobites, as the supporters of the now exiled king were called. The 1689 session of parliament remains notable mainly for the fact that the Test Act of 1681, to which Argyll had adhered only 'as far as it is consistent with itself and the Protestant religion' was repealed. Two days later, on 16 March, the reading of letters from the two kings who were rivals to the Crown destroyed the cause of James VII & II. While William wrote in conciliatory terms, promising to defend the Protestant faith, James declared open vengeance on all those who foreswore his allegiance, thereby implying that, in the event of his reinstatement, he would give preference to those who supported his own Roman Catholic religion.[1]

Thanks to the tactlessness and stupidity of his letter, many of his supporters deserted him. Foremost amongst those who at this point left the parliament were the Duke of Atholl and Lord Balcarres, who formed a rival convention at Stirling. Another who deserted the Edinburgh parliament was John Graham of Claverhouse, he who was known for his handsome countenance as 'Bonnie Dundee'. Still agile at the age of forty-one, he climbed the castle rock to persuade the Roman Catholic Duke of Gordon to continue holding Edinburgh Castle for King James. Dundee was declared a rebel by the Edinburgh Convention on 30 March. He then rode to his own house of Dudhope, in Angus, where, in great secrecy, he began to organise a rising to restore the exiled king. A few days later, at the beginning of April, he raised his standard for King James on Dundee Law. Some seven weeks later, by 25 May, Dundee had amassed an army of about 2,000 men, raised mostly from the Highland clans. Colin, Lord Balcarres, still loyal to King James, rather than to the man who commanded his army, was one of the few from the Lowlands who rallied to his cause.

Once again the castle of Balcarres echoed to the sound of shouted orders and the tramp of marching feet. To Countess Anna the noise must have been ominously reminscent of the days forty-six years earlier, when she had seen Colin's father, Alexander, auburn-haired as his son, ride away to fight for the Covenant army against what they had then both believed to be the unjust persecution of their Presbyterian faith by King Charles I.

On 27 July, Dundee won an outstanding victory at the head of the Pass of Killiecrankie. But in the moment of triumph, having dismounted to water his horse, he was killed by a sniper's bullet. Bereft of his leadership, the Jacobite army was defeated, largely by a force of Covenanters, at Dunkeld. As news drifted in of the outcome of the battle, Countess Anna waited in great fear to hear her son's fate. Her relief can be easily imagined when she heard that he had survived, apparently unwounded, to be taken as a prisoner to Edinburgh Castle. Subsequently released, he took refuge in Holland, thus following in the footsteps of his father and mother who, summoned there by King Charles II in the freezing winter of 1654, had left him and his brother at Balcarres in the care of the good Mr Forret when he himself had been just eighteen months old.

The death of Dundee and the subsequent defeat of his army at Dunkeld all but ended the resistance to King William in Scotland. At the instigation of the Master of Stair, Secretary of State for Scotland, the Highland chiefs swore allegiance to William at the end of December 1692, with, as is so well known, the one exception by default, of MacDonald of Glencoe.

*

By the end of 1690 Countess Anna, thanks to her good management, had written off the loans which she had made to her son, Colin Balcarres. Nonetheless, despite her reduced income, she managed to provide a dowry for his daughter, her granddaughter and namesake, Anna (known as Lady Elizabeth Lindsay), when the latter married the Earl of Kellie in 1690.[2]

Despite her concern for her son, whose future seemed so insecure, Countess Anna was oppressed with a still greater sorrow on her mind. This was accentuated when, some time about the year 1697, the philosopher Richard Baxter's posthumous biography was published. Baxter was the man to whom she had gone in desperation, begging him to reason with her seventeen-year-old daughter Anne, then determined to become a Roman Catholic. Much as she had once admired

Baxter, Anna was greatly hurt by his assertion that her daughter's doubts concerning the creed of the Anglican Church were 'pretended'. More distressing still was his claim that she had lied over her disappearance and would soon return. He also wrote that, on reaching France, she had told the queen mother, Henrietta Maria, that her own mother 'had used her hardly in religion'.[3] In a word, wrote Baxter, 'her mother told me that before she turned Papist she scarce ever heard a lie from her, and since then she could believe nothing of what she said'.[4]

It was now some years since Mr John Makgill, the minister of Cupar, had visited Anne in the convent in Paris, where, as Sister Anna Maria, she lived. He had found her 'a knowing and virtuous person [who] had retained the saving principles of our religion'.[5] She had died, apparently in the convent, during Baxter's lifetime, having never seen her mother since that fateful moment thirty-six years before when, leaving her house in London, she had disappeared in a coach. A servant sent in pursuit who had caught up with the coach in Lincoln's Inn Fields had been assured by Anne that 'she merely went to see a friend and would return', this being taken by Baxter as proof of her capacity for telling lies. Countess Anna who, at the prompting of her first husband, had read all Baxter's previous books with such avidity, now could not forgive him for maligning her dead daughter's name. In a faltering hand, she wrote in the margin of the page in his book which contained his allegations against her, 'I can say with truth, I never in all my life did hear her lie, and what she said, if it was not true, it was by others suggested to her, as that she would come back on Wednesday; she believed she would, but they took her, alas! from me, who never did see her more.'[6]

Although she was so much saddened and angered by Baxter's seemingly unwarranted and undeserved attacks on her long-lost eldest daughter, Countess Anna had two out-standing reasons for happiness during her last years. One was the return of her son Colin, Lord Balcarres, to Scotland in the winter of 1700.

It transpired that Colin had actually walked from Utrecht to the Hague, a distance of about fifty miles. There he had put his case for returning home to the Reverend William Carstares, the Royal Chaplain, who was a neighbour in Fife. Carstares approached King William who, told that Balcarres was now so poor that he had to walk instead of ride, said, 'If that be the case let him go home; he has suffered enough.'[7]

The joy of Countess Anna in having her son returned to her was matched only by that of the company of her grand-daughter, Anna. 'Lady Betty' as she was affectionately known, the eldest daughter of Colin Balcarres, was then about thirteen or fourteen. By the year 1700 Earl Colin had been married no fewer than four times. Following the death of his first wife, the tragic little Mauritia de Nassau, he had then married Jean Carnegie, daughter of the Earl of Northesk some time between 1672 and 1680. Elizabeth, born in 1680, was their only child, which suggests that her mother, like her predecessor, died in childbirth, as so frequently happened at that time. Colin then married another Jean, this time Lady Jean Kerr, daughter of Sir William Kerr, who became the 2nd Duke of Roxburgh. By her he had two children, Colin and Margaret. However, Lady Jean also died and Colin had since married a fourth time, to Lady Margaret Campbell, daughter of the Earl of Loudoun, before he was taken prisoner in 1689. Lady Margaret must have joined him in Edinburgh Castle, where he was held as a political prisoner, for two sons, Alexander and James, both of whom would succeed him as 4th and 5th earls of Balcarres, were born before the end of 1691. There being no mention of her joining him in Holland, one presumes that she stayed in Scotland until he returned home.

Meanwhile we have it on Lord Lindsay's word that Earl Colin's eldest daughter lived, it would seem on a permanent basis, with his mother in Balcarres Castle. History was repeating itself to the extent that Anna's affection for her was deepened by the similarity of their circumstances. Lady Betty was, in fact, only a little older than Anna had been when, on the death of her father, she had gone all the way from the castle of Brahan, in Ross-shire, to live with his cousin the Earl of Rothes in Leslie Castle.

Lord Lindsay describes Lady Betty as 'glancing like a beam of light (as is the wont generation after generation, in such old houses), with her bright smile and her waving hair, through the wainscoted chambers and across the sun-flecked corridors of Balcarres'. Continuing, he writes that: 'The last notices that I have of the aged friend of the elder and younger Lauderdale, of the Rothes of 1648, and of Sir Robert Moray, are mixed up with accounts incurred, in June 1706, for a silk lutestring gown, bought by her as a present for little Elizabeth, and with an additional provision for her of a thousand marks, dated the 1st of October that same year, in token of "the singular love, favour and affection we have and bear to the said Lady Elizabeth, our grandchild".'[8]

Lord Lindsay does not mention it but a list of household expenses of the year 1696, in addition to many articles of clothing, includes 'three books of Virgil and gramer' at the cost of £9, together with 'a wig for Lord C' at £15 16/, which may be an indication that Anna was also looking after her grandson, Colin, who, born some time in the early 1680s, would then have been about fifteen years old. The purchase of volumes on Latin and grammar, together with 'a bag to carie his books' certainly suggests that his grandmother was sending him off to university, most likely to St Andrews, which was so conveniently close. Sadly this young Colin, who became ADC to the Duke of Marlborough, was to die in 1708.

Lord Lindsay mentions that in June 1706 Countess Anna had written her name with a faltering hand. By October, however, it was firm again, but now she was eighty-five, a great age for those times, and indications are that she had suffered a stroke or else had become debilitated in some other way common to advancing years. Anna died at Balcarres, it would seem in 1707. All that is known for certain is that she was buried beside her first husband, her dear Gossip, whom she had so greatly loved, and their son Charles, who for so brief a time had been the 2nd Earl of Balcarres before dying at the age of twelve.

Born in 1621, in the reign of James VI & I, Anna lived through the reigns of four Stewart kings and one who, although his mother was the daughter of Charles I, and his wife a daughter of James VII & II, was of Dutch nationality. Finally, in 1702, she had seen the ascension of another daughter of the Stewart King James, in the person of Queen Anne. Her death marked the end of an era for, in the following year, Scotland lost her own parliament for nearly 300 years when the Treaty of Union with England was signed in 1707.

*

It is difficult to reconstruct both the character and appearance of someone who lived and died so long ago. Nonetheless, contemporary descriptions show a woman of exceptional virtue and integrity, level-headed and practical, who was steadfast in her loyalty to those with whom she was connected both through relationship and acquaintance, and to causes in which she believed. Countess Anna, renowned as she was for her beauty, was also remarkable for her intelligence at a time when education was considered to be largely the prerogative of men. In addition, she was highly respected for her honesty, in particular for the remarkable consistency with which, throughout her many tribulations, she remained steadfast in her devotion to religion, as embodied in the Presbyterian Kirk.

Her piety and at the same time her down-to-earth common sense were remarked upon, and in some cases proved inspirational, to the largely profligate courtiers who, both in France and Holland, peopled the courts of the then-exiled Charles II and his mother, Queen Henrietta Maria. Countess Anna had no reason to love those people, particularly the queen mother who had 'stolen' her daughter to Catholicism in every sense of the word. Nonetheless she showed them great tolerance, refusing to castigate what to her must have been intolerable hypocrisy, in either letter or word. So great was the impression made by her character that, in the years when she followed her husband on the Continent, she was described as the most stable influence of the court.

She endured heartbreaking sorrow, upheld by her stoic faith. The death of her first two boys as babies was, perhaps, made the more bearable by the fact that infant mortality was then accepted as almost inevitable for want of medical knowledge. The loss of Charles, however, whom she had found so brimming with health on her return to Balcarres after an absence of seven years, following so closely on that of his father, is known to have tried her to the limits of her mental and physical strength.

The 'murder' by execution of her second husband, Archibald Argyll, and the cruelties inflicted on her in prison, when she was already over sixty, as verified by her daughter Henrietta, were trials which would have destroyed most women. Anna, however, survived, immersing herself in the work of saving her outlawed son's forfeited estate in Fife.

Had she lived in more peaceful times, Anna would have been conspicuous if only for her charming personality and her lovely face. The strength of her character might, under these circumstances, have remained unrevealed except to her family

and closest friends. As it was, thanks to the very severe trials
which she endured, she emerges, as if from a chrysalis, as a
woman of enormous courage and honesty, whose will and
Christian spirit could not, under any circumstances, be subdued.

From the records of the seventeenth century, describing
dreadful disease and devastating civil war, she emerges as
someone outstanding. First as the beautiful girl, then as the
wife adored by the young husband whom she loved so much in
return. Later she is proved to have been the invaluable support
of her second husband, an insecure, taciturn man. Finally,
following his death, she became the matriarch, strong and
protective to all the members of her family. 'My care hath been
great for you', as she wrote to her son Colin in conclusion of
her long letter of advice on his first marriage to the ill-fated
Mauritia de Nassau.

To her children and grandchildren she ever resembled the
rock in a storm-strewn ocean on whom, when assailed by their
own difficulties, they could always rely and safely turn to for
advice. Henrietta, who was particularly devoted to her mother,
summed up her feelings for her in the already quoted passage
of her diary in which she wrote that she considered herself
blessed to have been 'trysted with so tender-hearted a mother',
who in her own life had set such an example that her children
and all those connected to her must follow it if only to be
dutiful and thankful as, despite her many trials and sorrows,
she herself had remained, 'to the great Giver of our mercies'.[9]

Notes

PART I

Chapter 1

1 MacKenzie. A., *History of the MacKenzies*, p. 245
2 Lindsay, Lord A., *A Memoir of Lady Anna MacKenzie, Countess of Balcarres & afterwards of Argyll, 1621–1706*, pp. 9–10
3 MacKenzie. A., p. 244
4 Ibid., p. 245
5 Lindsay, Lord. A., p. 10

Chapter 2

1 Buchan, J., *Montrose*, p. 74
2 Donaldson, G., *The Edinburgh History of Scotland*, vol. 3, p. 311
3 Ibid., p. 311
4 Marshall, R. K., *The Days of Duchess Anne*, p. 98

Chapter 3

1 Buchan, J., p. 69
2 Ibid., p. 72
3 Ibid., p. 73
4 Ibid.
5 Ibid., p. 79
6 Donaldson, G., p. 321
7 Ibid.

8 Buchan, J., p. 95
9 Leslie, John, Earl of Rothes, *A relations of proceedings concerning the affairs of the Kirk of Scotland, from August 1637 to July 1638*, p. 169
10 J. & J. Keay, *Encyclopedia of Scotland*, pp. 616–17
11 Buchan, J., p. 101

Chapter 4

1 Lindsay, Lord A., p. 11
2 Ibid., p. 12
3 Ibid., p. 13
4 *Burke's Peerage*, p. 616
5 Lindsay, Lord A., pp. 50–1
6 Ibid., p. 13
7 Ibid., p. 14
8 Ibid., p. 115
9 Ibid., pp. 50–1
10 Ibid.

Chapter 5

1 Lindsay, Lord A., p. 22
2 Wedgwood, C.V., *The King's War 1641–1647*, p. 555
3 Buchan. J., *Montrose*, pp. 210–11
4 Wedgwood, C.V., p. 611

231

Chapter 6

1 Wedgwood, C.V., *The King's War, 1641–1647*, p. 555
2 Lindsay, Lord A., p. 24
3 Ibid.
4 Wedgwood, C.V., p. 611

Chapter 7

1 Lindsay, Lord A., p. 27
2 Ibid., pp. 29–30
3 Ibid., pp. 28–31
4 Ibid., p. 29
5 Ibid., pp. 29–30
6 Ibid., pp. 28–31

Chapter 8

1 Lindsay, Lord A., p. 31
2 Willcock, J., *A Scots Earl*, p. 41
3 Ibid., p. 42
4 Ibid., p. 44
5 Campbell of Airds, Alastair, *A History of Clan Campbell*, vol. 2, p. 264
6 Ibid., p. 265
7 Ibid.
8 Lindsay, Lord A., p. 39
9 Willcock. J., p. 49
10 Lindsay, Lord A., p. 31
11 Campbell of Airds, Alastair, *A History of Clan Campbell*, vol. 3, p. 266
12 Lindsay, Lord A., p. 32
13 Ibid., p. 32
14 Ibid., p. 46

Chapter 9

1 Lindsay, Lord A., p. 32
2 Ibid., pp. 32–3

3 Ibid., p. 33
4 Ibid., p. 33
5 Campbell, Alastair of Airds, vol. 2, p. 270
6 Lindsay, Lord A., p. 35
7 Fraser, Antonia, *King Charles II*, p. 137
8 Lindsay, Lord. A., p. 35
9 Ibid., p. 35
10 Ibid.
11 Ibid., p. 39
12 Ibid.
13 Ibid.
14 Ibid., p. 40
15 Ibid., p. 43
16 Ibid.
17 Ibid.
18 Ibid., p. 44

Chapter 10

1 Lindsay, Lord A., pp. 46–7
2 Ibid., pp. 47–8
3 Ibid.
4 Ibid., p. 48
5 Ibid., p. 34
6 Ibid.
7 Ibid., p. 50
8 Ibid., p. 111
9 Marshall, Rosalind K., *The Days of Duchess Anne*, p. 151
10 Lindsay, Lord A., p. 46
11 Ibid., p. 49
12 Fraser, A., p. 195
13 Lindsay, Lord A., p. 57
14 Ibid., p. 52
15 Ibid., pp. 52–3
16 Ibid., p. 63
17 Ibid., p. 54
18 Ibid., p. 55

Notes

Chapter 11

1 Lindsay, Lord A., p. 58
2 Ibid., pp. 58–9
3 Ibid., pp. 60–2
4 Ibid., p. 63
5 Ibid.

Chapter 12

1 Lindsay, Lord A., p. 66
2 Donaldson, G., *The Edinburgh History of Scotland*, vol. 3, pp. 263–5
3 Lindsay, Lord A., pp. 66–7
4 Ibid., p. 69
5 Ibid., p. 70

6 Ibid., pp. 70–2
7 Ibid., p. 72
8 Ibid., p. 72
9 Ibid., p. 74
10 Ibid., p. 75
11 Ibid., pp. 76–7
12 Ibid., pp. 77–8
13 Ibid., pp. 78–9
14 Ibid., p. 82

Chapter 13

1 Lindsay, Lord A., p. 83
2 Ibid.
3 Ibid., p. 84
4 Ibid., p. 85
5 Ibid., pp. 88–95

PART 2

Chapter 14

1 RCAHMS, *Stirlingshire*, vol. 2, pp. 277–84
2 Bowie, William, et al, *The Black Book of Taymouth*, p. xx. Also Willcock, J., *A Scots Earl*, pp. 5, 7
3 Willcock, J., *A Scots Earl*, pp. 431–2
4 Lindsay, Lord A., pp. 150–1

Chapter 15

1 Lindsay, Lord A., pp. 99–105
2 RCAHMS, *Stirlingshire*, vol. 2, pp. 277–284
3 Lindsay, Lord A., p. 100
4 Ibid.
5 Ibid., p. 104
6 Ibid., p. 111
7 Ibid., p. 112

Chapter 16

1 Willcock, J., *A Scots Earl*, p. 213
2 Burnet, G., *Bishop Burnet's History of His Own Time*, vol. 1, p. 418

Chapter 17

1 Fraser, A., pp. 355–6
2 Ibid., p. 372
3 Willcock, J., *A Scots Earl*, pp. 227–9
4 Ibid.
5 Ibid., pp. 232–3
6 Ibid.
7 Fraser, A., p. 182
8 Campbell, Alastair of Airds, vol. 3, p. 350
9 RCAHMS, *Argyll*, vol. 1, p. 160
10 Ibid., p. 184
11 Lindsay, Lord A., p. 115
12 Ibid., p. 249
13 Willcock, J., p. 249

PART 3

Chapter 18

1 Balffour Paul, Sir James (ed)
   The Scots Peerage, vol. 1, p. 337;
   also Campbell, Alastair of
   Airds, vol. 2, p. 12
2 Willcock, J., *A Scots Earl*,
   p. 252
3 Ibid., p. 256
4 Ibid., p. 257
5 Ibid., p. 259
6 Ibid., p. 261
7 Ibid., p. 263
8 Ibid., p. 264

Chapter 19

1 Willcock. J., p. 270
2 Ibid., p. 271
3 Ibid.
4 Ibid., p. 274

5 Ibid., p. 276
6 Ibid., p. 271–2
7 Ibid., p. 274
8 Ibid., p. 276

Chapter 20

1 Willcock, J., p. 272
2 Lindsay, Lord A., pp. 116–7
3 Ibid.
4 Ibid.
5 Ibid., p. 118

Chapter 21

1 Willcock, J., p. 291
2 Ibid., p. 294
3 Fraser, A., p. 324
4 Ibid., p. 409
5 Willcock, J., pp. 302–3
6 Ibid., p. 298

PART 4

Chapter 22

1 Fraser, Lady Antonia, *King
   Charles II*, p. 427
2 Willcock, J., p. 132
3 *Register of the Acts of the Privy
   Council*
4 Lindsay, Lord A., p. 124
5 Ibid.
6 *Register of the Acts of the Privy
   Council*; also *Fountainhall's
   Decisions*, vol. 1, p. 251
7 Ibid.
8 Lindsay, Lord A., pp. 124–5
9 Carstares State Papers, p. 196

10 Carstares State Papers, p. 119;
   also Willcock, J., *A Scots Earl*,
   pp. 316–18

Chapter 23

1 Lindsay, Lord A., p. 122
2 Willcock, J., p. 330
3 Ibid., p. 331

Chapter 24

1 Willcock, J., p. 328
2 Ibid., p. 335. The quote within
   this is taken from the *Narrative
   of Patrick Hume*.
3 Ibid., p. 336

Chapter 25

1 *Diary of Lady Henrietta Campbell: Fountainhall's Decisions*, vol. 1, p. 362
2 Willcock, J., p. 400
3 Ibid., p. 393

Chapter 26

1 *Records of the Burgh of Glasgow, 1663–90*, pp. 375–6
2 Willcock, J., *A Scots Earl*, p. 400
3 Lindsay, Lord A., p. 128

Chapter 27

1 Campbell of Airds, A., vol. 3. p. 53
2 Lindsay, Lord A., p. 129
3 Willcock, J., *A Scots Earl*, pp. 414–5
4 Lindsay, Lord A., p. 129
5 Ibid., p. 131
6 Ibid.
7 Ibid.
8 Willcock, J., *A Scots Earl*, p. 417
9 Ibid., p. 132
10 Ibid., p. 133

Chapter 28

1 Lindsay, Lord A., p. 135
2 Ibid., p. 136
3 Previous to the ascension of William of Orange there had only been one king in Scotland called William, namely William I, known as William the Lion (1165–1214)
4 RCAHMS, *Argyll*, vol. 7, p. 225
5 Ibid.
6 Lindsay, Lord A., p. 137
7 RCAHMS, *Argyll*, vol. 7, p. 316; also information from Sir Ilay Campbell, Bt of Succoth and Crarae
8 Lindsay, Lord A., p. 137

Chapter 29

1 Ferguson, W., *The Edinburgh History of Scotland*, vol. 4, p. 3
2 Ibid., p. 139. Anna was Earl Colin's daughter by his second marriage, to the daughter of Lord Northesk. He was to marry four times in all. See *Burke's Peerage* under Earls of Crawford and Balcarres.
3 Lindsay, Lord A., p. 140
4 Ibid.
5 Ibid.
6 Ibid.
7 Ibid., p. 138
8 Ibid., p. 141
9 Diary of Lady Henrietta Lindsay, wife of Sir Duncan Campbell of Auchinbreck

Bibliography

Primary Source

1 The Letters of Lady Anna MacKenzie, Countess of Balcarres and afterwards of Argyll. Entrusted to the National Library of Scotland by the Earl of Crawford and Balcarres.

Secondary Sources

Ashley, Maurice, *James II*, J.M. Dent & Sons Ltd, 1977

Balfour Paul, Sir James (ed.), *The Scots Peerage*, Vol. 1, D. Douglas, Edinburgh, 1904–14

Bowie, William, et al, *The Black Book of Taymouth*, ed. Cosmo Innes, Bannatyne Club, Edinburgh, 1855

Buchan, John, *Montrose*, Thomas Nelson & Sons Ltd, London & Edinburgh, 1928

Burnet, Gilbert, *Bishop Burnet's History of His Own Time*, Vol. 1, 1724

Campbell of Airds, Alastair, Unicorn Pursuivant, *A History of Clan Campbell*, Vols 2 & 3, Edinburgh University Press, Edinburgh, 2002 & 2004

Carstares State Papers

Donaldson, Gordon, *The Edinburgh History of Scotland*, Vol. 3, Mercat Press, Edinburgh, 1965

Ferguson, W., *The Edinburgh History of Scotland*, Vol. 4, Mercat Press, Edinburgh, 1987

Firth, C.H. (ed.), *Scotland and the Commonwealth: Letters And Papers Relating To The Military Government Of Scotland, From August 1651 To December 1653*, new edition: Kessinger Publishing, LLC, Montana (USA), 2007

Fraser, Antonia, *King Charles II*, Weidenfeld & Nicolson Ltd, London, 1979

Fry, Michael, *The Scottish Empire*, Tuckwell Press & Birlinn, Edinburgh 2001

Gillies, The Revd W. A., *In Famed Breadalbane*, Clunie Press, Perthshire, 1938

Gleeson, Janet, *The Arcanum*, Bantam Books, 1998

Gregory, Donald, *History of the Western Highlands and Isles*, William Tait, Edinburgh, 1836

Keay, John & Julia (eds), *Encyclopaedia of Scotland*, Harper Collins, London, 1994

Lenman, Bruce, *The Jacobite Risings in Britain 1689–1746*, Scottish Cultural Press, St Andrews, 1980

Leslie, John, Earl of Rothes, *A relation of proceedings concerning the affairs of the Kirk of Scotland, from August 1637 to July 1638*, ed. David Laing, Bannatyne Club, Edinburgh, 1830

Lindsay, Lord Alexander, *A Memoir of Lady Anna MacKenzie, Countess of Balcarres & afterwards of Argyll, 1621–1706*, Edmonston & Douglas, Edinburgh, 1868

MacKenzie, Alexander, *History of the MacKenzies*, A. & W. MacKenzie, Inverness, 1894

Marshall, Rosalind K., *The Days of Duchess Anne, Life in the Household of the Duchess of Hamilton 1656–1716*, Collins, London, 1973

Records of the Burgh of Glasgow, 1663–90

Register of the Acts of the Privy Council

Royal Commission on the Ancient & Historical Monuments of Scotland (RCAHMS), *Stirlingshire*, Vol. 2, HMSO, Edinburgh, 1963

Royal Commission on the Ancient & Historical Monuments of Scotland (RCAHMS), *Argyll*, Vols 2 & 7, HMSO, Edinburgh, 1974 and Glasgow, 1992

Spalding, John, *The History of the Troubles and Memorable Transactions in Scotland and England, from MDCXXIV to MDCXLV*, Vol 1, Bannatyne Club, Edinburgh, 1828

Stevenson, David, *Alasdair MacColla and the Highland Problem in the 17th Century*, John Donald Publishing Ltd, Edinburgh, 1980

Wedgwood, C.V., *The King's War 1641–1647*, Collins, London, 1958

Willcock, J., *The Great Marquess: Life and Times of Archibald, 8th Earl and 1st (and only) Marquess of Argyll, 1607–1661*, Oliphant, Anderson & Ferrier, Edinburgh, 1903

— *A Scots Earl in Covenanting Times: Being Life and Times of Archibald 9th Earl of Argyll, 1629–1685*, Andrew Elliot, Edinburgh, 1907

Index